Design an Construction

The terms 'sloop' and 'frigate' derived from the days of sailing ships. A frigate was a square-rigged warship, smaller than a line of battle ship, with a single continuous gun deck; in effect, they performed the duties of the modern cruiser. The sloop was smaller, originally single-masted but growing in size until they stood just below a frigate in the order of battle. Both terms were re-introduced by the Royal Navy in the twentieth century, albeit for rather different roles.

The First World War 'Flower' class, based on mercantile scantlings and ordered in 1915, were classed as 'fleet sweeping sloops', reflecting their initial use; the later vessels, ordered in 1916 and 1917, were reclassified as 'convoy sloops', following the Admiralty's reluctant introduction of a convoy system. The design of sloops between the two World Wars led to a more general-purpose emphasis, with greater anti-air (AA) and anti-submarine (ASW) capability, but it was not until the early years of the Second World War that the minesweeping requirement was removed. The term Sloop was officially dropped in 1937, although it remained in common usage, and the vessels rated as either Escort Vessels, Patrol Vessels or Minesweepers.

At the beginning of the Second World War, there was marked shortage of destroyers, A large building programme was undertaken, but destroyers were expensive, took a long time to build, could only be built by a limited number of shipyards and were in great demand to support the work of the fleet and carry out offensive actions against the enemy. It was necessary to produce more escorts to protect the ships of the Merchant Navy and these had to be cheaper, quicker and easier to build so that they could be constructed by a greater number of shipyards with limited (or no) experience of building warships. The best-known design was that of the Flower class corvettes (see ShipCraft Special) but their limited seaworthiness underlined the need for larger ships. The term 'frigate' was introduced with the 'River' class launched between 1942 and 1944, after their initial classification as Twin-Screw Corvettes. The new category referred to vessels larger than corvettes but smaller than destroyers and not mounting torpedo tubes, with emphasis on anti-submarine capability. It was applied to subsequent escort classes like the 'Loch/Bay' group and also the ex-US destroyer escorts of the 'Captain' class.

SLOOPS

As the sloops of the First World War started to wear out towards the end of the 1920s, the Admiralty began to consider replace-

Opposite: Bridgewater, pre-war at Malta, clearly showing the two tall pole masts, the aft LA 4in gun mounting and the minesweeping davits at the stern. (Author's collection)

Below: Penzance in 1931 shows a very similar appearance to that of Bridgewater in Malta. It clearly shows the difference between the forward HA 4in gun mounting and the aft LA mounting.

ments, their intention being to build two prototypes, one with steam turbine machinery and one with diesel engines, but as no suitable British diesel engines existed, this idea was dropped. Shallow draught was considered a necessity for their main role of minesweeping, even though this was a handicap for asdic operations. No asdic sets were available at that time however, although most sloops received Type 127 by the beginning of the war, and this was usually replaced by Type 144 when a Hedgehog mortar was fitted.

The two ships of the *Bridgewater* class, *Bridgewater* and *Sandwich*, were both built by Hawthorn Leslie and launched in 1928. At 266ft 4in loa, with a beam of 34ft 1in, they were intended for minesweeping, a large minesweeping winch being fitted aft, and carried two 4in and two 3pdr saluting guns. Initially fitted with just two depth charge chutes and 4 depth charges, at the beginning of the Second World War, they carried 15 depth charges but this was increased to a maximum of 80 by the end of the war.

Only the forward 4in Mark V gun was suitable for use against aircraft, but shortly before the Second World War, the aft mounting was replaced with a second HA mounting and the saluting guns were replaced with quad 0.5in machine guns. In turn these were later replaced with 20mm Oerlikon guns, two in 1942 and four in 1943, when a Hedgehog mortar was also fitted.

The twin-shaft machinery installation, comprising two Admiralty 3-drum boilers and two Parsons geared steam turbines producing 2000shp, gave the vessels a top speed of 16½ knots.

These two ships were followed by the *Hastings* class of four vessels – *Folkestone*, *Hastings*, *Penzance* and *Scarborough* – with the same hull dimensions and machinery installation, all being launched in 1930. Their armament and depth charge arrangements were the same and were similarly increased just prior to and during the Second World War. *Folkestone*, *Hastings* and *Scarborough* each received two quad 0.5in mountings early on. *Folkestone* did not have her 4in LA mounting changed to HA until the middle of 1941, when she also received two 20mm guns, as did *Hastings*. *Scarborough* did not receive her 20mm guns for another year, but then had two more added a few months later. *Folkestone* also had two additional 20mm mounts added in 1942, when her 0.5in guns were removed.

Only *Folkestone* (1942) and *Scarborough* (1943) received the Hedgehog mortar. Apart from *Penzance*, which had been sunk in 1940, the others received radar Type 286M in 1941, this being replaced by Type 271 during the following year. HF/DF was fitted during 1943.

As well as minesweeping, *Hastings* was able to carry out minelaying. She could accommodate 18 to 22 mines.

A 'tropicalised' and lengthened version for India, *Hindustan*, was launched in the same year. She received two 20mm guns in 1942. India also received another sloop, *Indus*, launched four years later, retaining the same length but with two 4.7in guns rather than 4in guns.

The hull of the *Hastings* class was lengthened by 15ft and the beam increased by 11in for the succeeding *Shoreham* class, which was built in two groups of four. The first four (*Bideford*, *Fowey*, *Rochester* and

Below: *Shoreham*, wearing a three-colour camouflage scheme, displays the two quad 0.5in gun mountings on a platform immediately aft of the funnel and 20mm guns in the bridge wings.

Shoreham) were launched in 1930/31, and the second group, frequently referred to as the Repeat *Shoreham* class (*Dundee, Falmouth, Milford* and *Weston*) in 1932. As built, the *Shoreham* class carried two additional 3pdr saluting guns but only one 4in LA mounting, the same propulsion system resulting in the same top speed. During 1938, the LA mounting was replaced by a HA mounting and a quad 0.5in mounting added.

During the Second World War, the saluting guns were either reduced in number or removed completely, a second quad 0.5in mounting fitted to *Fowey, Rochester* and *Shoreham*, and up to six 20mm guns (*Fowey*) added. The number of depth charges carried was increased up to a maximum of 90, and *Fowey* and *Rochester* were fitted with a Hedgehog mortar. They received radar Type 286 early in the war, this being upgraded to Type 271/291 and HF/DF fitted as opportunities arose.

The Repeat *Shoreham* class, with the exception of *Falmouth*, were initially fitted with two 4in guns – a HA mounting forward and a LA mounting aft. A HA mounting was fitted aft and a quad 0.5in mounting added just before the war. *Dundee* was lost in 1940 but the others received a second quad 0.5in mounting, with 20mm guns being added later.

Eight ships were built of the following *Grimsby* class (*Aberdeen, Deptford, Fleetwood, Grimsby, Leith, Londonderry, Lowestoft* and *Wellington*) when the hull length was reduced to that of the *Hastings* class but the beam increased to 36ft. Four further vessels were built in Australia for the Royal Australian Navy. The well-proven machinery installation was retained, still resulting in a top speed of 16½ knots.

With this class, the emphasis began to move away from minesweeping and greater consideration was given to the role of escort, resulting in the design armament

being two 4.7in/45 Mark IX LA mountings, a 3in 20cwt HA mounting and four 3pdr saluting guns. *Grimsby* was completed with minelaying sponsons at each quarter. Minelaying required a reduction in top weight, including the removal of 'X' gun. The minelaying facilities were removed later and a minesweeping winch and related equipment installed.

However, all the ships did not complete with the design armament, *Fleetwood* being fitted with two twin 4in/45 Mark XVI guns rather than single mountings. As AA defence increased in importance, the calibre of the preferred gun became 4in rather than 4.7in. The shells were much lighter and easier to handle, and the increased rate of fire more than made up for the reduction in explosive weight.

The mixture of single 4in HA and LA mountings and/or twin 4in mountings varied considerably in the vessels of this class, as did the removal of the 3in HA mounting, the addition/removal of quad 0.5in mountings and addition of 20mm guns. *Aberdeen* and *Deptford* received their Hedgehog mortars in 1942, but *Fleetwood, Leith, Londonderry, Lowestoft* and *Wellington* did not receive this equipment until 1943.

The installation of radar and HF/DF equipment also varied widely with time, although all, except *Lowestoft*, had HF/DF by the end of 1942. *Deptford, Fleetwood, Leith, Londonderry* and *Lowestoft* all received Type 286 in the early days of the war and all had Type 271 by the end of the war, *Londonderry* and *Lowestoft* also receiving Type 291.

There was a brief deviation from the main development path when, in 1933, orders were placed for the six vessels of the *Kingfisher* class – *Kingfisher, Mallard, Puffin, Kittiwake, Sheldrake* and *Widgeon*. These were intended as coastal escorts, suitable for replacing the old ships used for

Above: *Kittiwake* in 1942 reveals the much lower profile of this class compared to the mainstream sloop development.

Below: *Puffin* shows a quad 0.5in mounting on the quarterdeck and two 20mm mountings on a platform just forward of it. Note the light frame structure at the fore end of the aft superstructure, supporting the communication aerials coming from the foremast.

fishery protection and anti-submarine warfare training in peacetime, while being suitable for mass production in wartime. They were just 243ft 3ins loa with a top speed of 20 knots, retaining two shafts and steam turbines similar to the other sloops. They were armed with a 4in/45 Mark V gun mounting and could carry a maximum of 60 depth charges, launched by two depth charge throwers and two depth charge chutes, with Type 124 sonar fitted in a retracting dome. No provision was made for minesweeping.

These were followed by three *Shearwater*

Above: *Enchantress* as an Admiralty yacht. The two single 4.7in gun mountings can be seen forward, as can the additional accommodation aft.

Left: *Enchantress* in April 1945 with the yacht accommodation aft removed. The after 4.7in guns were never mounted but the ship carried a 12pdr AA gun on the quarterdeck. The single 20mm in the bridge wings and the radar 'lantern' atop the bridge are very evident.

class (*Guillemot*, *Pintail* and *Shearwater*) of similar design and armament but 10ft shorter overall. The vessels' original anti-aircraft armament comprised eight Lewis guns, but most vessels, in both classes, had two single 20mm guns added sometime during the Second World War.

Bittern, *Enchantress* and *Stork*, the three ships of the *Bittern* class, had lengthened hulls, similar to those of the *Shoreham* class, but with two feet greater beam. Increased power resulted in a top speed of 18½ knots and *Enchantress* was fitted with Brown-Curtis, rather than Parsons, turbines.

The design armament was four 4.7in single mountings (two forward and two aft) but *Bittern* completed with three twin 4in/45 Mark XVI HA mountings. *Bittern* was fitted with fin stabilisers to improve the performance of the Director Control Tower on the bridge for control of AA fire, but this was not entirely successful. She also received a quad 0.5in mounting as built but was lost before any additions could be made.

Enchantress was completed as an Admiralty yacht with additional accommodation replacing the aft gun mountings and *Stork* as a survey ship without any armament. *Enchantress* did receive a 3in/12pdr HA gun in 'Y' position, two 20mm guns on the bridge wings and two quad 0.5in mountings in 'X' position at the outbreak of war, the latter being replaced by two additional 20mm mountings in 1943. A vertical

HF/DF pole mast was also fitted adjacent to the quad 0.5in mountings and an air warning radar Type 286 fitted at the mast head.

Stork was re-armed as *Bittern* prior to the war, initially receiving four 20mm guns, a short lattice mast aft for a surface warning radar, the Type 286 radar being fitted at the mast head. Later a lattice mast, carrying both radar antennas, replaced the foremast and the aft mast was removed. At the end of the war she had no 0.5in or 20mm mountings but three 40mm mountings. Both *Enchantress* and *Stork* received Hedgehog mortars in 'B' position in 1942, *Enchantress* receiving HF/DF at the same time but *Stork* did not receive her HF/DF equipment until 1943. Later, both sloops had Type 286 radar replaced by Type 291.

The three ships of the following *Egret* class (*Auckland*, *Egret* and *Pelican*) were 10 feet longer and fitted with four twin 4in/45 Mark XVI mountings and a quad 0.5in mounting. The aft 4in mounting displaced the usual minesweeping winch. Only one HA.DCT was fitted and so the mountings were forced to operate in local control if more than one target was to be engaged. Installed power was increased to 3600shp, resulting in a top speed of 19½ knots.

Single 20mm guns were added in the bridge wings early in the war but *Auckland* was lost early before receiving any further changes. The other two received a second 0.5in mounting which was later replaced by additional 20mm guns. *Egret* received

Below: This view of *Auckland* in December 1938 clearly shows the basic control system for the twin 4in gun mountings.

Hedgehog in 1942, but *Pelican* did not receive hers until 1944, when she underwent a major refit, which also included the replacement of one 4in mounting by a quad 2pdr mounting. This was the first class to be fitted initially with tripod masts which were later replaced by short lattice masts. Both *Egret* and *Pelican* received radar Type 286 during 1941, and had it replaced by Type 271 in 1942 and 1943, respectively, when HF/DF was also fitted.

Four similar vessels were also built for the Indian Navy but they only carried six, instead of eight, 4in guns.

The four sloops of the *Black Swan* class – *Black Swan*, *Erne*, *Flamingo* and *Ibis* – were seven feet longer than the *Egret* class but retained the same beam. Armament was reduced to three twin 4in/45 Mark XVI mountings, a minesweeping winch being installed on the quarterdeck. However, a 2pdr mounting 'M' Mark VII was installed amidships for close-range AA defence. Depth charge arrangements were increased to two depth charge throwers, two depth charge rails and three depth charge chutes. Each rail could accommodate 12 depth charges and 7 spare depth charges were stowed in the vicinity of each thrower. Provision was also included for laying mines, there being capacity for 32 Mark XV mines. All minesweeping equipment, except the winch, had to be removed to accommodate the alternative configurations.

Installed power was further increased to 4300shp, increasing maximum speed to 19½ knots, and Denny-Brown stabilisers were fitted to all four vessels. *Black Swan*, *Erne* and *Flamingo* received Hedgehog during 1942 and single 20mm guns were added at various times, the final outfit usually comprising six mountings. *Black Swan* had two twin and two single 20mm mountings in mid-1945.

The escalating demand for enhanced armament, including an increase in the number of depth charges carried on deck, and sensors, often requiring stronger masts, resulted in a large increase in topweight, and therefore reduced stability. The Modified *Black Swan* class, the largest class of sloops to be built, therefore received an additional one foot beam. The requirement for minesweeping was deleted, the design concentrating on AA defence or anti-submarine warfare to protect merchant ships in convoy.

The *Black Swan* class were launched in 1939 and 1940, but the earliest of the modified sloops was not launched until the middle of 1942 and the last one not until 1946. All were fitted with three twin 4in/45 Mark XVI mountings but the initial AA armament varied considerably, reflecting the changes in design and availability of the smaller calibre gun mountings over the completion period of four years. Those intended primarily for anti-submarine

Above: *Pelican* in November 1946 shows her outfit at the end of the war with a quadruple 2pdr pom-pom replacing the twin 4in gun mounting in 'X' position. Note the enhanced director control tower compared with that in the previous photo of *Auckland*.

Right: *Black Swan* in 1942/3 shows the minesweeping winch on the quarterdeck replaced by a quadruple 2pdr gun mounting.

Below: In this photo, *Woodcock* is fitted with twin 40mm guns on the platform aft of the funnel and twin 20mm guns on the quarterdeck. It also shows the arrangement of depth charge throwers and rails on the quarterdeck.

warfare received a Hedgehog mortar on completion.

For example, when first completed in September 1943, *Starling* was fitted with three 4in twin H/A L/A Mark XVI guns on Mark XIX mountings, four twin Oerlikon guns (two on a platform amidships and two on the quarterdeck), two single Oerlikon guns (on sponsons at the Signal Deck level), four depth charge throwers and two depth charge rails. HMS *Kite* completed slightly

before *Starling* and received two quadruple 'pom-pom' mountings in lieu of the twin Oerlikon mountings amidships. When *Amethyst* completed in March 1944, she was fitted with two single Oerlikon guns instead of the twin mountings on the midships platform and a two-part Split Hedgehog mortar forward on the Signal Deck.

All vessels were fitted with Types 271 and 291 radars, and those without

Left: The forecastle of *Banff* shows the open 5in gun together with the two 6pdr mountings.

Hedgehog also received a Type 285 gunnery radar.

Ten US Coastguard cutters of the 250ft long 'Lake' class launched between 1927 and 1931 were transferred to the Royal Navy under lend-lease arrangements in the middle of 1941, becoming known as the *Banff* class. These were single-shaft, steam turbine powered vessels with a maximum speed of 17 knots. Originally armed with one 5in/51, one 3in/50 and two 6pdr gun mountings, they soon received four additional single 20mm mountings. Two were mounted forward of the superstructure and two aft, although arrangements varied in detail. Later they were fitted with air warning radar on the mast and surface warning radar on the bridge roof. In some, the 3in gun was replaced by a British 12pdr.

FRIGATES

The term 'frigate' was re-introduced to the Royal Navy with the 'River' class, which were built in Great Britain, Canada and Australia. A total of 134 vessels were built, with Australia building four more to a slightly modified design. The first vessels were launched in the middle of 1942 and the last, an Australian built vessel, in 1945. In the early stages of the design, they were referred to as 'twin screw corvettes'.

When asked for comments as to how to improve the 'Flower' class corvettes, Smith's Dock, the originators of the design, produced a ship that was 320ft long and had two sets of corvette machinery but the same weapons. The naval constructors produced the design of a slightly shorter vessel, 300ft overall. Good seakeeping was an important requirement, resulting in a design with significant flare and sheer at the bow and a long forecastle.

The Director of Naval Construction (Stanley Goodall) was concerned that the vessels should be simple to build and seven shipbuilders, all of whom had been closely associated with the construction of the 'Flowers', were approached. Charles Hill of Bristol was selected to lay off the design in their mould loft and supply the hull data to the others. Smith's Dock was to prepare detailed drawings of the keel framing, bulkheads and deck layouts; Fleming & Ferguson on Clydeside were to draw the mountings for the machinery; Henry Robb of Leith would design the bridge, mast and some of the accommodation, the remainder to be by Charles Hill; A & J Inglis concentrated on the smaller items.

All but five received two sets of machinery the same as that of the 'Flower' class (but with water-tube boilers), the five being *Cam*, *Chelmer*, *Ettrick*, *Halladale* and *Helmsdale*, who received Parsons geared turbines resulting in an increase in top speed of one knot for these vessels.

Originally intended to mount just one 4in gun, it was decided to increase this to two. These were simple Mark XIX guns with limited range and capability and no form of fire control was fitted. Generally, this was an unpopular choice but economy was key at the time. The frigates' main role was to be ASW and so little thought was given to AA protection. The early intention was to fit single 2pdr pom-pom mountings but production difficulties with the desired mark of mounting, the Mark VIII*, led to the decision to fit twin powered Oerlikon mountings Mark V. But there were production difficulties with this mounting also, and so most of the 'Rivers' completed with four single 20mm Oerlikon mountings, two on the bridge wings and two aft. There was provision to fit up to ten 20mm guns but this was never achieved.

After the launch of the first few vessels it was decided to fit a Hedgehog mortar but too late for the first frigate, *Rother*, that was completed without. The mounting was fitted on the foredeck, immediately aft of the breakwater. Two depth charge rails, each with 15 charges, were fitted at the stern and four depth charge throwers on each side, giving the capability to launch a 14-charge pattern.

HMS *Rother* trialled the asdic Type 128 in April 1942 and it was decided to fit the improved Type 144 as standard in the 'River' class. Similarly, following trials of radar Type 271 in the 'Flower' class corvette *Orchid*, it was decided to fit the equipment, with its rotatable aerial and narrow beamwidth, to the 'River' class as soon as possible.

The first twenty frigates were fitted with a full range of minesweeping gear – Mark 1 Oropesa sweep, LL magnetic sweep and SA acoustic sweep – but this was removed in 1942 to accommodate the maximum number of depth charges.

A large number of the 'River' class were built in Canadian shipyards and operated by the Royal Canadian Navy, when they carried names of towns and cities, frequently with a twin 4in Mark XVI mounting forward, although remaining under the designation of 'River' class. They were built in shipyards either on the west coast or the St Lawrence River, being too large for the St Lawrence canal system, which excluded shipyards on the Great

Right: The French ship *L'Aventure* (ex-'River' class HMS *Braid*) wears a small pennant number on her bow.

Below: *Nith* in 1943 highlights the two single 4in gun mountings and the radar on the bridge before the tripod foremast.

Above: This aerial shot of *Perim* in August 1944 gives a clear indication of the upper deck layout of the 'Colony' class frigates.

Lakes which had built many 'Flower' class corvettes.

When the United States entered the war, they also had a shortage of suitable escort vessels and so 10 of the 'River' class were to be built by Canadian Vickers for use by the USN, under a 'reverse' lend-lease arrangement. Only two were actually supplied to the USN, *Asheville* (PF-1) and *Natchez* (PF-2), and these were fitted with three US 3in guns instead of the British 4in guns. The third mounting was fitted on the forecastle. They also carried two twin 40mm mountings at the break of the forecastle and four single 20mm mountings.

A contract was awarded to the naval architects Gibbs and Cox to produce an all-welded version, suitable for pre-fabrication and mass production. The main visual difference of the resulting *Tacoma* class was a rounded bridge with portholes rather than the squared off bridge of the British frigates. A contract for twenty-one was given to the Walsh-Kaiser shipyard in Providence, Rhode Island, for transfer to the Royal Navy. They were built with phenomenal speed and formed the 'Colony' class in British service.

These were armed as the American *Asheville* and *Natchez*, and consideration was given to replacing the 3in guns by 4in guns but it was thought the structure would not stand the increased recoil forces.

The Royal Navy 'Captain' class actually consisted of two groups, all provided under 'lend-lease' arrangements by the United States. The first group of 32 were taken from the *Evarts* class of destroyer escorts and the second group of 46 from the *Buckley* class. Both classes had two shafts, the *Evarts* class driven by General Motors V12 diesels and the larger *Buckley* class by General Electric turbines to produce top speeds of 20 and 24 knots, respectively. In both cases these power generators drove electric motors rather than driving the shafts directly via gearboxes, due to there being a shortage of gearboxes, but the system also gave an improved response. The *Evarts* class destroyer escorts were 289ft 5ins oa with a 35ft 2in beam, and the *Buckley* class 306ft oa with 37ft beam.

As designed, the *Evarts* class did not carry torpedo tubes and the torpedo tubes of the *Buckley* class were removed on arrival in Great Britain, thus receiving the designation 'frigate' in Royal Navy service. The US quad 1.1in gun mountings, where fitted, were normally removed before the vessels sailed to Great Britain and were replaced by a mixture of 20mm and 40mm guns, depending on what was available at the time.

A number of other modifications were carried out on arrival at Pollock Dock, Belfast, primarily in order to reduce the violent rolling motions caused by the high level of stability resulting from the reduction in top weight. More depth charges were stowed on the upper deck and the bilge keels were enlarged.

The most noticeable difference between RN and USN designs was the relative standards of accommodation – bunks and cafeteria messing for the crew and cabins in the superstructure for the officers in US built ships. The CPOs and POs shared a mess which had separate sleeping and living

Above: *St Helena* in September 1944, with two 3in guns forward, a Hedgehog mortar immediately aft of the forward mounting, two 20mm guns in the bridge wings and two more on the deck immediately below, two twin 40mm guns at the break of the forecastle, the aft 3in mounting and three more single 20mm guns on a platform at the forward end of the quarterdeck.

Below: The ex-*Evarts* class destroyer escort HMS *Drury* in June 1943 shows 'splayed' depth charge rails, contrary to RN practice where they were usually arranged parallel to the centreline.

Above: The ex-*Buckley* class destroyer escort HMS *Holmes* has a 2pdr 'bow-chaser' gun mounted right forward for use combatting the German *schnellboote*.

Left: This very clear view from aft of the *Buckley* class destroyer escort USS *Liddle* (DE-206), shows the torpedo tubes which were removed from ships transferred to RN service, hence the classification 'frigate' rather than 'destroyer'. The quad 1.1in mounting and its director, which were also removed, are just aft of the tubes.

quarters, including armchairs, a sofa and a refrigerator! On the other hand, toilet facilities were very primitive, without even any screening being present between those using the 'two-seater trough' and those using the washbasins.

In addition to the quad 1.1in mounting, the *Buckley* class was fitted with three 3in/50 Mark 22 mountings, two 20mm guns forward of the bridge and two amidships, a Hedgehog mortar, eight depth charge throwers and two depth charge rails. Some of the class received a twin 40mm mounting in lieu of the quad 1.1in mounting. The *Evarts* class were similarly armed but with just one 20mm mounting forward of the bridge. The 3in guns were manually operated with a rangefinder and director on the bridge providing range and bearing information. This equipment was omitted for most vessels transferred under lend-lease. The 40mm or 1.1in mounting was remotely controlled from a second director.

As the 'River' class were too long to be built by many of the shipyards that had built corvettes, the 'Castle' class was designed by Smith's Dock Company, the same shipyard that had designed the 'Flowers'. With a length of 252ft oa, they were approximately 50 feet longer than the 'Flower' class and 50 feet shorter than the 'River' class. They had a beam of 36ft 8ins and retained the single shaft machinery installation of the 'Flowers', also maintaining the same top speed of 16½ knots.

The bridge reflected the latest 'naval'

type of structure and a lattice mast was fitted. A total of forty-four ships were completed, all being launched in 1943 and 1944. Ten were transferred to Canada and one to Norway, with five completing as rescue ships. Fifteen orders were cancelled in Great Britain as were all the thirty-six orders given to Canada.

They were armed with a single 4in gun, the Mark XIX gun on a Mark XXIV mounting replacing the 4in Mark IX on a CP mounting of the 'Flower' class. AA armament was increased to two twin and two single 20mm Oerlikon guns. The biggest differences were in the anti-submarine weapons, a Squid mortar replacing Hedgehog and the number of depth charges being reduced with just two throwers and a single rail.

The 'Loch' and 'Bay' classes, a development of the 'River' class, used a common hull form, 307ft oa and 38ft 7ins beam, and a common machinery installation, twin-shaft vertical triple expansion engines with two Admiralty 3-drum boilers giving a maximum 5500ihp for a speed of 19½ knots. Two of the 'Loch' class, *Loch Arkaig* and *Loch Tralaig*, were fitted with Parsons geared turbines which resulted in a slight increase in maximum speed to 20 knots. The two classes differed in armament, the 'Lochs' concentrating on the ASW role and the 'Bays' emphasising the AA role.

There was a total of thirty 'Loch' class vessels, three of which were operated by the Royal Canadian Navy, three by the South African Navy and two were completed as

Below: *Lancaster Castle* at anchor shows the naval style bridge and the lattice mast with radar at the top. The three short barrels of the Squid A/S mortar are poking over the surrounding bulwark on the deck above the 4in mounting.

Above: This photo of *Loch Fada*, taken in the 1960s, shows the arrangement of the twin Squid installation, aft of the 4in mounting.

Below: A weather-beaten *Loch Gorm* in 1945 retains the quadruple pom-pom on the aft end of the superstructure, covered to protect it. She wears the remains of a Western Approaches type camouflage.

depot ships. They were launched between 1943 and 1945 and more than 50 further vessels were cancelled.

The primary gun armament for the vast majority of the class was a single 4in Mark V gun on a Mark XXIV mounting, only *Loch Veyatie*, the last to be completed, being fitted with the later Mark XXI gun. For close range defence they were fitted with a quadruple 2pdr pom-pom and four 20mm guns, this number frequently increasing in service, up to a maximum of ten. A twin 40mm mounting was originally specified but production shortages resulted in its replacement by the pom-pom. *Loch Craggie*, *Loch Eck* and *Loch Glendhu* were fitted later with two 40mm guns, reducing the number of 20mm guns carried and the three South African vessels were later fitted with six 40mm guns and all the 20mm guns were removed.

The most important enhancement was in the fitting of a twin Squid ahead-throwing ASW installation in lieu of Hedgehog. Each Squid mounting could fire three large depth-fused bombs, compared to the much smaller 24 contact-fused bombs of Hedgehog, at greater ranges. The increased effectiveness of this installation resulted in a reduction in the number of depth charges carried, there being only two throwers and a single rail to launch them. The two Squid mountings were fitted forward of the bridge and the 4in gun on a bandstand aft of the breakwater. The Asdic equipment was also improved.

The class was designed for rapid mass production and included a number of features to assist with this, including the forward sheer being comprised of three straight lines rather than a continuous curve. A lattice mast was fitted to accommodate the heavier radar systems, and they were provided with a 27ft whaler and a 25ft motor boat.

The nineteen vessels in the 'Bay' class were all laid down as 'Loch' class frigates but the need for greater AA protection in the Pacific resulted in significant changes in the armament to meet the threat. The twin Squid installation was replaced by a single Hedgehog mortar, once again located on the forecastle. The number of depth charges was increased and the vessels received four throwers and two rails.

The primary gun armament was two twin 4in Mark XVI mountings, one forward and one aft. Fourteen of the class received remote power control installations, but shortage of control equipment resulted in the others receiving the three-man rangefinder director. Four single 20mm guns were fitted and two twin 40mm mountings at the break of the forecastle.

The 'Bay' class were all launched in 1944 and 1945. One ship was cancelled, four were completed as survey ships and two as despatch vessels.

Below: *St Austell Bay* in 1945 clearly show the aft twin 4in gun mounting and the two twin 40mm mountings at the break of the forecastle. Note the short HF/DF mast just forward of the 4in mounting.

Model Products

GHQ – USA   1:2400 Scale

For wargaming, models need to be of small scale to enable representable ranges without occupying large areas, of robust construction and with sufficient detail to enable swift recognition of vessel type. The American company GHQ produce the Micronaught series at 1:2400 and this includes models of both the Evarts and Buckley class destroyer escorts. These are made of pewter and are unpainted. The series come in 'bubble' packaging on a colourful card, three identical models being supplied on each card. For wargaming, the models can just be painted grey with a few highlights, but some enthusiasts will prefer to paint them in a camouflage pattern.

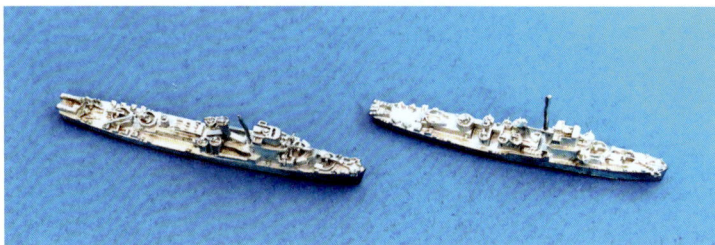

NAVIS-NEPTUN – GERMANY   1:1250 Scale

Ship recognition models are produced at the internationally accepted scale of 1:1250 by many manufacturers. The most prolific warship manufacturer is Navis-Neptun, the models generally being painted grey with some highlights, such as black funnel tops and brown tops to the boats. Currently, two models of US ships supplied under lend-lease are available from Navis-Neptun: NN1350, the *Evarts* class DE, and NN1351, the *Buckley* class DE. There are also two models of British ships available: NN1180, a 'River' class frigate, and NN1184, a *Shoreham* class sloop (below right).

A reasonable amount of detail is included on these white-metal models, such as the depth charge rails and stowages and antennas and crowsnest on the mast. With such a wide range of vessels being produced, it is inevitable that only a limited number are available at any one time.

SEA VEE MODELS – FRANCE   1:1250 Scale

Sea Vee Models are hand assembled and painted by Sean Pritchard. They are more detailed, often being painted in camouflage schemes, and offer the opportunity to 'personalise' individual vessels in the same class. As an example, the photo shows K428 *Loch Alvie* and K620 *Loch Gorm*. Also shown is K355 *Hadleigh Castle*; note the inclusion of decals for the pennant numbers and the etched brass masts.

SPIDERNAVY – USA   1:1250 Scale

Spidernavy produce four different models of sloops: HMS *Starling*, a modified *Black Swan* class sloop, 1943 SN 2-01; *Egret*, 1939 SN 2-02; *Ibis*, *Black Swan* class sloop, 1941 SN-Liz-1183; HMS *Erne*, *Black Swan* class sloop, 1942 SN-Liz-1183a.

EAGLE – UK
1:1200 Scale

■ Eagle plastic kits ceased production as long ago as the 1960s but kits do appear on eBay and other similar sites from time to time. In their 'Battle of the Atlantic' series, Eagle included models of the *Allington Castle* and *Balfour* of the 'Captain' class (Kit No 3), and *Peacock* of the *Black Swan* class (Kit No 4). Each kit contained a

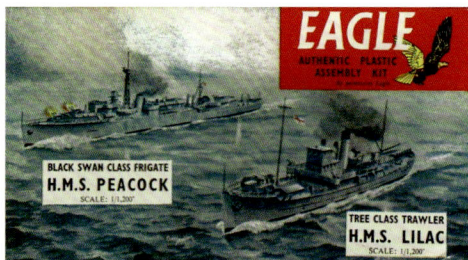

full-hull, split at the waterline, superstructure moulding(s) and a sprue with the fine details attached. Stands were also included for the display of full-hull models. Instructions were limited to one assembly diagram and the painting instructions suggested black for gun barrel tips, propellers and funnel tops and silver flor searchlights and reflectors.

IPMS(UK) FINE WATERLINE SPECIAL INTEREST GROUP – UK
1:700 Scale

■ The Fine Waterline SIG released a limited number of 'semi-kits' including a *Shoreham* class and a *Grimsby* class sloop (see photo), and a 'Castle' class frigate. These kits were intended for 'skilled' modellers and included a resin waterline hull and mouldings for the funnel and main superstructure. The 'Castle' class model also included a small sheet of etched brass for the lattice mast.

Instructions were simple and started with some historical information highlighting some of the many changes, primarily to armament, that these ships underwent during their careers. A list suggested possible sources for the many small detailed parts (such as guns and boats) not included. With the large number of 'after-market'

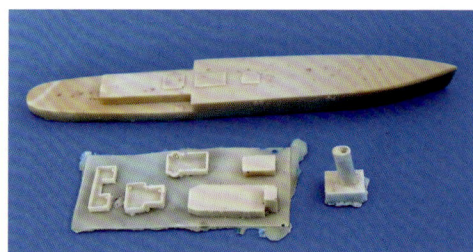

accessories available from a range of manufacturers most of the required items could be readily purchased, but a small amount of 'scratch-building' was still necessary.

These basic sets of resin mouldings provided the basis for some models not available from any of the major manufacturers.

IMPERIAL HOBBY PRODUCTIONS – USA
1:700 Scale

■ This model of HMS *Wild Goose* comprises a resin hull and superstructure with some smaller details provided in white metal. There is also some brass rod and a decal sheet with hull pennant numbers. Instructions are simple and begin with an introduction to the original vessel,

followed by a drawing of the parts, some general words on assembling resin kits and a general arrangement drawing of the sloop as in 1943 (not to scale). There then follows two assembly drawings and some painting instructions. The introduction mentions changes to the vessel during her career and the second assembly drawing notes the option of 20mm or 40mm guns, but the general arrangement drawing does not show these and so some research is necessary to identify the exact locations.

AJM MODELS – POLAND
1:700 Scale

■ The models of *Black Swan* and *Ibis* are similar but do highlight the many differences between vessels in the same class at different dates in their careers. The most obvious differences between these two are the minesweeping winch on the quarter-deck of *Black Swan* and the many more light AA guns carried by *Ibis* later in the war, as well as her colourful camouflage scheme.

The models come in stout cardboard boxes, with the resin waterline hull protected by 'bubble-wrap', the resin components in one plastic bag and the etched brass sheets and decals in another. The instructions are supplied on three double-sided A4 sheets, with 11 assembly diagrams for *Black Swan* and 16 for *Ibis*. The majority of resin components are provided on resin sprues, with just the hull and larger superstructure parts moulded separately. There is just a small amount of 'flash' that needs to be removed and cleaned-up, but the separate parts do have substantial 'pours' that need to be removed carefully.

The two hulls are virtually identical and include lots of moulded detail such as deck planking, bollards and fairleads. The differences come in the moulded locations for deck components, such as the minesweeping winch. The larger of the two etched brass sheets are different for each vessel, and include items such as guardrails, ladders, davits, anchors and anchor chains. The smaller ones are identical and include just three shields for the twin 4in gun mountings. The decal sheet

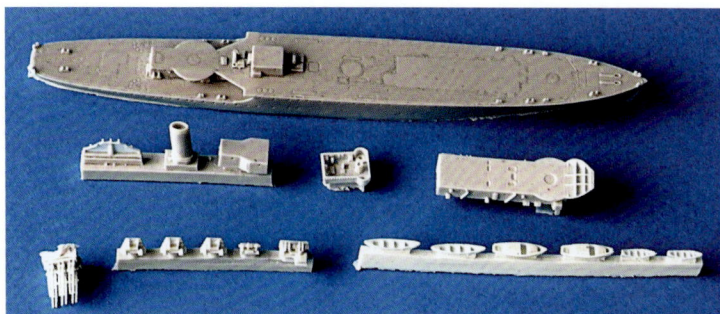

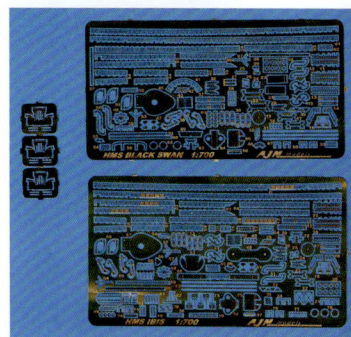

contains two different sizes of white ensign, a union jack for those who want to represent the sloop at anchor, and draught marks in both black and white.

To complement the many differences between the two sloops, colour schemes are shown, the recommended paints coming from Lifecolor. *Black Swan* is just a simple grey 507C but *Ibis* has a complicated camouflage pattern that is different on each side.

Two well detailed kits that, with patience and care, will result in impressive models.

ATLANTIC MODELS – UK
1:700 Scale

■ This kit of HMS *Gorleston* includes a resin waterline hull with no superstructure but a considerable amount of moulded detail, including the depth charges in rails at the stern and those stowed adjacent to the depth charge throwers. The other resin components are moulded on three sprues, the first containing the two larger superstructure parts, the funnel and forward gun platform. The second sprue, which is duplicated in order to provide all the parts required, contains the ship's boats, Carley rafts, depth charge throwers, small guns and cowl vents, two different types being

provided in order to enable the modeller to produce models of different vessels in the same class. The third sprue contains the main armament, the director platform, the crowsnest and the radar lantern.

The etched brass sheet includes railings and splinter matting, gun shields, davits, boat details, depth charge rails and supporting assemblies for rafts and gun platforms. There is a length of brass rod for the mast. Instructions come on three sheets of A4, two being double-sided, and include a camouflage pattern for the vessel as in 1943, paints being specified from the Colourcoats range. This drawing includes the pennant number 'Y92' but no decals are supplied.

As mentioned above, alternative parts are supplied to allow models of different vessels to be built, but it is for the modeller to research precise details and colours.

Atlantic Models have included two models of the *Black Swan* class sloops *Amethyst* (ATK 700-061) and *Starling* (ATK 70042) in their list of intended releases for 2020.

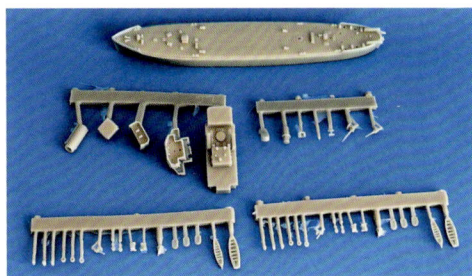

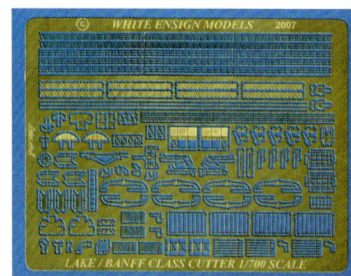

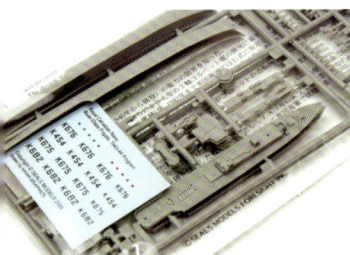

SEALS MODELS – JAPAN

1:700 Scale

■ This plastic kit of a 'River' class frigate was supplied in a plastic bag and contained a two-part hull, split lengthways, with a large forecastle deck and a smaller quarterdeck. All the parts were contained on a single sprue. Detail was limited and there was some flash. The model was identified as being from the 1943–44 programme of the Royal Canadian Navy and appropriate decals were included.

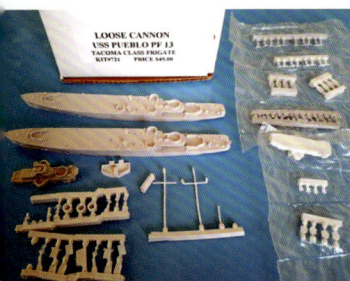

LOOSE CANNON PRODUCTIONS – USA

1:700 Scale

■ Now out of production, in the early 2000s Loose Cannon Productions released a resin kit of USS *Pueblo*, one of the *Tacoma* class frigates. An etched brass sheet was also included and instructions came in the form of two written sheets and a sheet of assembly diagrams. One unusual feature for vessels in this scale is that the etched brass sheet included the tackle to be spread between the davits and the boats were hung from the tackle.

Although marketed as *Pueblo* (PF-13) the instruction sheet not only contained details for this vessel in Ms 22 camouflage but also for USS *Rockford* (PF-48) in Ms 32 camouflage.

SKYWAVE PIT-ROAD – JAPAN

1:700 Scale

■ The box (SPW22) contains three identical, light grey sprues, each of which can be assembled as either a *Cannon* class or *Buckley* class destroyer escort, both classes having the same hull dimensions. There is a double-sided instruction sheet with three assembly diagrams, for each class. The sheet also includes a list of the vessels in the class with their pennant numbers, including those of the 'Captain' class. There is also a double-sided colour sheet, featuring two colour schemes for each class.

There is a decal sheet including six sets of white numbers with black shading, in two different sizes, and six sets of small white numbers. Only the latter ones are referred to on the drawings, and they are shown as black! – although photographic evidence does show white to be correct. There are numerous aircraft decals for both British and American aircraft, but there are no aircraft in the kit! There is no etched brass.

The waterline hull is moulded with the deck as one piece, and a separate waterline plate. The mouldings are clean but do have large attachment points to the sprue, which will need careful cleaning. There is a reasonable amount of detail moulded on to the sides of the superstructure but the lines of the whaler are very fine compared with those in the other kits.

This model will benefit greatly from the use of etched brass and after-market resin replacement parts.

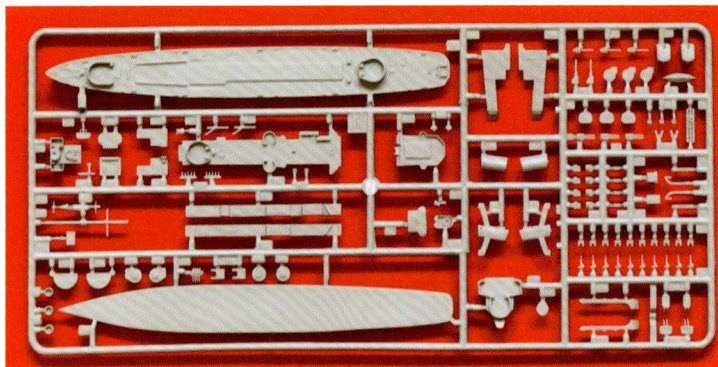

NIKO – POLAND

1:700 Scale

■ This model of the USS *Gendreau*, a *Buckley* class destroyer escort, comprises a resin waterline hull, two plastic bags of resin mouldings and a sheet of etched brass. The hull is finely moulded and just needs a little cleaning up along the waterline. The details moulded in place include the spray shields alongside the superstructure, complete with freeing holes at deck level, and two rows of depth charges at the stern. One bag contains the bridge and a sprue with the funnel and torpedo tubes attached, and the other four sprues with gun mountings, a boat and other details attached. These details are easily dislodged from the sprues and some will be found loose in the bag. There is a little flash, particularly around the gun mountings with their very fine barrels.

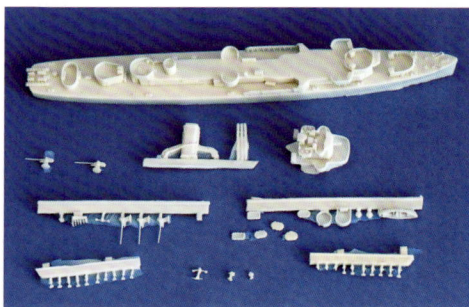

The etched brass sheet does not include any railings but does include the depth charge rails and stowages, ladders, 20mm and 1.1in gun mountings, davits, life raft supports, details for the 3in guns and the mast. The instructions include two sheets of assembly drawings, one covering the hull with the locations of all the parts and the other the assembly of the various etched brass parts. The reverse side of the first sheet contains a 1:700 scale general arrangement drawing and a camouflage drawing of the *Gendreau*, with paint colours specified from the Humbrol range. The pattern is different on each side and the deck also has an interesting pattern.

A well produced kit that is capable of resulting in a fine model.

SKYTREX – UK   1:600 Scale

Skytrex produced a number of white metal models in a Coastal Forces series, including the 'Captain' class HMS *Bentinck* (CF39). These were advertised as being at a scale of 1:600 but the waterline length of this model scales more closely to 1:700. The kit comprises a waterline white metal casting with integral superstructure and details, the only separate parts being three gun mountings and a tripod mast, although the spaces between the legs of the tripod are obscured with white metal.

There are no assembly instructions, just

a short background to the class, displacement and maximum speed.

A crude model intended primarily for wargaming.

BLACK CAT MODELS – FRANCE   1:400 Scale

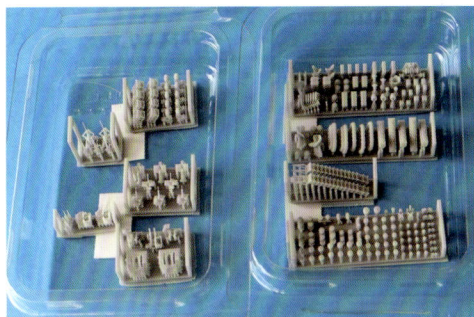
RIVER CLASS FRIGATE

This full-hull model of a 'River' class frigate was released in February 2020. The scale of 1:400 is popular in Europe, particularly France and Poland, although 1:350 is more normally recognised as an international standard. The hull and super-structure, together with some larger fittings, are moulded in resin, although smaller fittings have been created using 3D printing techniques. Although moulded in resin, full advantage has been taken of the original computer model in the instruction booklet. One point of interest is that the boats are moulded in resin, whereas the same company uses 3D printing techniques for their range of accessories, including boats, at 1:350 scale.

The hull needs a little cleaning up along the keel line but is otherwise very clean, as are the superstructure parts. The other resin mouldings are on substantial sprues. The 3D printed parts are very detailed and clean, as to be expected. In addition, there are some lengths of rod, of different diame-

ters for the mast, a sheet of etched brass, including guardrails, and a sheet of decals, comprising numbers and the letter 'K', permitting the modeller to choose the vessel to be modelled.

As well as computer modelling, the 16-page A5 instruction booklet makes good use of colour. On page 16 is K370 in camouflage. Although not identified, K370 was HMS *Windrush*.

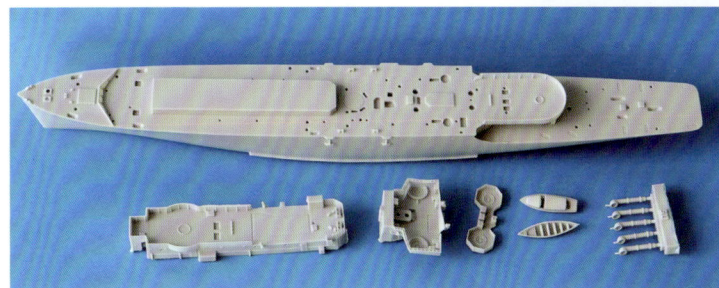

STROMBECKER MFG CO – USA   1:360 Scale

This rather unusual model of a *Buckley* class destroyer escort dates from 1949 and is made of Western Pine Wood. Inside the box are three pre-shaped pieces of wood – the base for the stand, a full-hull (purists may question the accuracy of the shaping, the deck line forward being much too full) and the main super-structure block. There is a sheet of veneer, with the shapes of platforms stamped on it

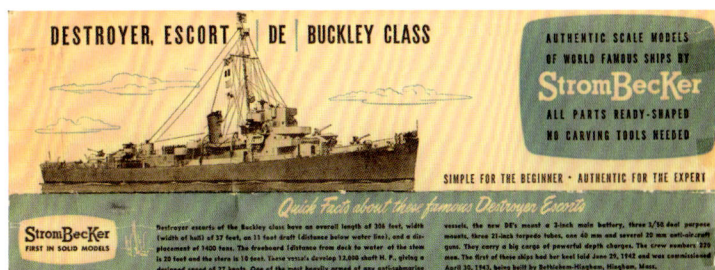

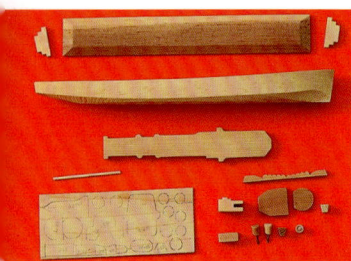

so that they can be separated from the sheet, and an envelope containing the smaller items. These include the upper parts of the superstructure, the funnel, dowelling for the mast, gun turrets, a piece shaped to represent the depth charges in their racks at the stern and the uprights for the stand. There is also a small sheet of sandpaper and an envelope containing Casco Powdered Casein Glue.

The publicity states that no carving is required but the instructions do call for some sanding and scratch-building, using the 'left-over' veneer. An interesting approach to modelbuilding before the days of plastic but not really a scale model.

ATLANTIC MODELS – UK
1:350 Scale

Having produced the masters for the resin kits for White Ensign Models, Peter Hall is now re-releasing them, along with his own models, all under the name of Atlantic Models. They include the sloops *Kittiwake* (ATK35061), *Amethyst* (ATK 35014), *Starling* (ATK35055), the ex-USCG cutter HMS *Gorleston* (ATK35065) and the frigate *Portchester Castle* (ATK35053).

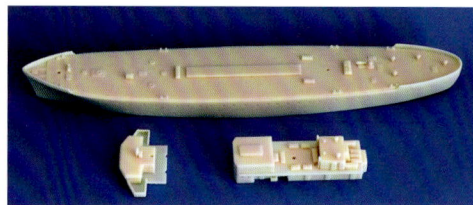

The format of all these models is similar – a resin hull, split at the waterline, resin superstructure and larger details, white metal guns and smaller details, an etched brass sheet, and extensive instructions. All the mouldings are well cast and require little cleaning up. Decals for pennant numbers are supplied with *Amethyst* but not with the others, although a sheet with a full range of letters and numbers, in varying colours, is available separately from the manufacturer.

The instructions include assembly and painting details for the selected vessel at a specific point in her career, but some of the kits do include optional parts so that the modeller can 'personalise' the model, either to represent the vessel at a different time in her career or to represent a sister vessel of the same class.

STARLING MODELS – UK
1:350 Scale

The model of HMS *Nadder*, a 'River' class frigate, has been produced taking maximum advantage of 3D computer modelling techniques. It is therefore very accurate (*eg* the fit of the superstructure over the raised coaming on the deck is superb) and it is a full-hull model.

The model comes well packed in a stout cardboard box, with the hull bubble-wrapped and the resin components in a plastic bag inside a smaller cardboard box. There is also an extensive etched brass sheet and a decal sheet of pennant numbers; black pennant letter K with six samples of each numeral, also black, in two different sizes (*ie* for the sides and the transom) and in two different fonts, one slightly 'wider'

Starling Models
STK03

HMS NADDER, RIVER CLASS FRIGATE

Resin and etched brass kit with turned brass parts and decals, full hull 1/350 scale

website - www.starling-models.co.uk
email - info@starling-models.co.uk

than the other. Six turned brass barrels are provided for the 4in, 20mm and 2pdr guns, and a tapered mast and yard.

Instructions are provided in a 12-page, A5 booklet which uses colour coding to help with the identification of the many resin and etched brass parts. Only one configuration is given, with the ship wearing a Western Approaches camouflage scheme. The instructions are extensive and deserve detailed study before construction commences.

Starling Models have included a model of the *Grimsby* class sloop, HMAS *Yarra* (STK08) and one of a 'Loch' class frigate (STK07), in their list of intended releases for 2020, together with a 1:700 scale model of the 'River' class frigate (STK09). The 3D CAD hull of *Yarra* is shown having additional details added before being used to create the master for the resin castings.

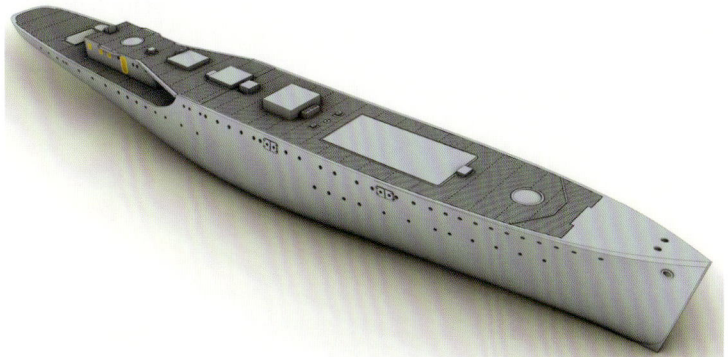

IRON SHIPWRIGHTS – USA

1:350 Scale

■ The review model of the *Buckley* class destroyer escort is an early release from Iron Shipwrights and so does not represent their current production methods and materials.

The box contains a waterline hull with approximately 3mm of excess resin on the bottom, which needs to either be removed or 'sunk' within a sea base. The upper part of the moulding is clean but there are inaccurate plating details moulded on the hull. The superstructure, funnel and other large parts, such as the boat, are moulded in resin, all with substantial pours which have to be carefully removed. The mast and other smaller details, such as torpedo tubes, guns and depth charge throwers are cast, rather indistinctly, in white metal.

There is an etched brass sheet from Tom's Modelworks which contains railings and netting, ladders, shields for 20mm guns, radar antenna, depth charge stowages and rails, gun depression rails, propeller guards and spray screens for the superstructure sides, the latter also being provided as resin mouldings.

Instructions are limited to a large, single side of very thick paper on which the resin and metal parts are identified and their locations shown. Part 6 is identified as an 'alternate gun tub', but no suggestions are given as to where it should be used. Assembly diagrams are included for the main superstructure and some of the etched brass assemblies. There are no decals and no colour details are included.

This is a model which requires a great deal of research and care in construction and will benefit greatly from the many after-market parts available.

Current releases from Iron Shipwrights include the destroyer escort USS *Evarts* (4-091) and the *Tacoma* class patrol frigate USS *Burlington* (4-081).

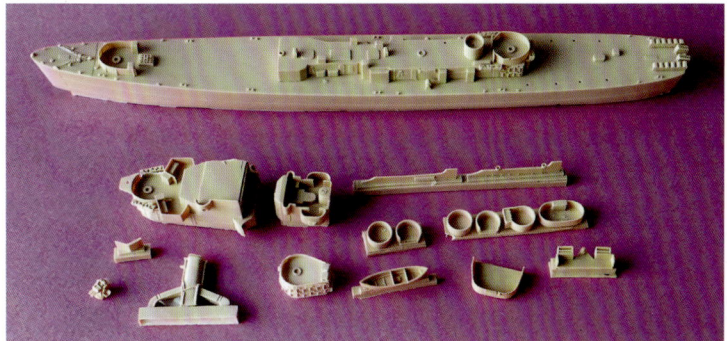

The box for *Evarts* contains a full-hull, complete with bilge keels and stern tunnels for the two shafts. The upperworks are cleanly moulded but the bottom is rather rough, particularly around the remains of the pour, and has a significant number of air holes. The hull is smooth with no plating details.

The smaller parts are contained in a plastic bag and have a lot of excess resin around them. The majority are just thin wafers but some of the superstructure parts show significant remains of the pour. Where the superstructure parts are attached to thin film, this is usually at the base and hence easily removed, but in some cases it is attached to the side, where there is moulded-on details also. The thin flash often completely surrounds the smaller parts, such as guns and propellers, and needs to be removed carefully, which is time consuming and requires concentration if the smaller parts are not to be damaged. The quality of the hull moulding compares favourably with that from European manufacturers but, as well as the excess flash, the smaller parts lack well defined detail.

There is an etched brass sheet by Tom's Modelworks containing 2- and 3-bar railings (but no netting), ladders, depth charge stowages and rails, propeller guards, radar antenna and 20mm gun shields. There are spray shields for the superstructure sides but the use of these will require the removal of the resin ones. The resin ones do not include the drainage holes at the deck edge, although there is an indication of their locations.

A general-purpose decal sheet is included, containing three different size

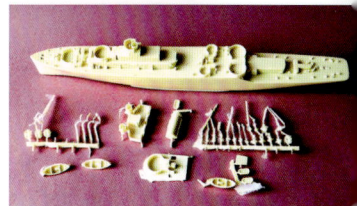

Top: *Buckley* class
Above: USS *Burlington*

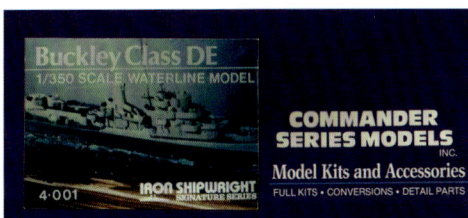

ensigns – Carrier/Battleship, Escort Carrier/Cruiser and Destroyer – together with aircraft markings. Two different sizes of hull numbers are included, in both black and white, but the instructions contain no suggestions as to their locations. There are ten single-sided pages of instructions. Page 2 identifies the resin parts and page 3 the brass ones. Assembly drawings are then given for the bow, midships and stern sections, and these are followed by assembly diagrams for the brass parts. Next is a clear general arrangement drawing for the vessel, including basic technical details, followed by a camouflage drawing. Finally,

there is a poor quality general arrangement drawing, identifying the locations of the components. This drawing carries a Tom's Modelworks logo, refers to the 'Captain' class frigates and does include some options, such as 40mm guns in lieu of the quad 1.1in mounting.

Inside the box lid, there are three lengths of brass rod attached, but there are no references to these in the instructions. Some further research is required to supplement these instructions in order to build an accurate model.

The kit of *Burlington* is very similar to that of *Evarts* and the comments similar but this kit has only four sheets of instructions. There are no general arrangement, camouflage or overall assembly drawings, and the two sheets of drawings are very sketchy, leaving the modeller to do a lot of research, and possibly modifications. The etched brass sheet does not appear to be from Tom's Modelworks – indeed the sizes of the parts supplied (*eg* 20mm gun shields, depth charge rails and stowages, height of railings) are different, but the decal sheets in the two kits are the same.

USS Evarts

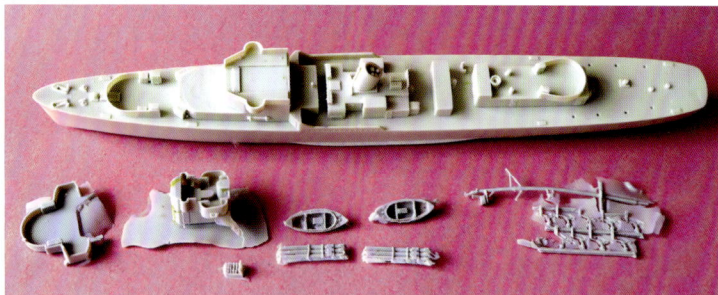

TRUMPETER – CHINA

1:350 Scale

The Trumpeter model of the USS *England*, a *Buckley* class destroyer escort, contains a four-part hull – deck, above-water, waterline plate and below-water – so that it can be constructed as a waterline or full-hull model. There are five light grey sprues, a stand for the full-hull model and three different types for the ship herself, one of them being duplicated. There is also a small etched brass sheet, some decals and an extensive set of instructions.

The instructions come in a 10-page booklet with 17 assembly diagrams and a colour drawing – although this is just a navy blue hull and superstructure, cocoa brown underwater and deck blue deck, the recommended paints being from Gunze Mr Color. The decals include white pennant

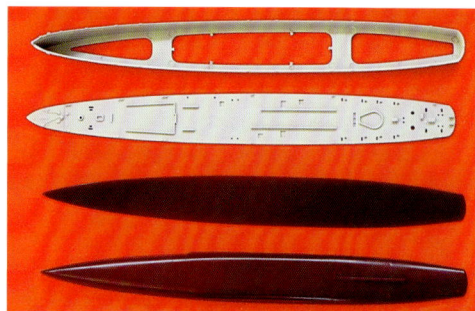

numbers, low down on the forward hull, and an ensign. The etched brass sheet includes depth charge rails and stowages, part of the Hedgehog mortar and a radar antenna, although the latter is also supplied in plastic.

The sprues are cleanly moulded with no flash but with plenty of detail, particularly on the sides of the superstructure. The fit of parts is very good so filler is seldom required. The duplicated sprue does provide a number of spare parts, such a set of propellers and a boat.

This is a first-class kit with the usual high quality expected from Trumpeter.

REVELL AG – GERMANY

1:250 Scale

Originally released in 1957, the model of USS *Buckley* has been re-released a number of times, the latest being in 2010, the only change being to the box art, although some new decals were introduced in 1964. The 'Captain' class HMS *Bligh* was released in 1997, with new instructions and decals, and a revised colour scheme, but no other changes. The kit comes in a flimsy cardboard box which opens at both ends –

not much use whilst building the model – with hull, deck and all the sprues in a single, large plastic bag.

The kit is of a full-hull model with a single piece hull. The hull has some plating lines on it with a few circles, presumably representing scuttles (port holes). The main deck and superstructure deck are also moulded in one piece with separate superstructure sides. The depth charges stowed on deck are moulded in place with separate mouldings for the depth charge rails. The superstructure sides have some basic detail moulded on them, with some of the doors left open, leaving a hole in the moulding, with the inside of the open door moulded on the superstructure side, adjacent to the hole. Lengths of oversize plastic guardrail stanchions are provided for the hull and stanchions are moulded at relevant locations on the superstructure. The instructions show the use of thread to represent the wires between the stanchions. The funnel is moulded in two halves, and the armament and other details are very basic and generally oversize. The decals include pennant numbers for the hull sides and a white ensign and there is the standard Revell paper sheet of signal flags, the same as included in their 1/700 scale kits!

Instructions are provided in an A4 size booklet which includes 25 assembly diagrams. The most useful diagrams are 26 and 27 which show the different camouflage patterns on each side of HMS *Bligh*. Significant work and replacement of parts/scratch building is required to produce an accurate model of a US DE, and even more for a RN 'Captain' class frigate. For a start, the keel needs to be extended aft, the bow profile corrected and bilge keels added to produce an accurate hull form.

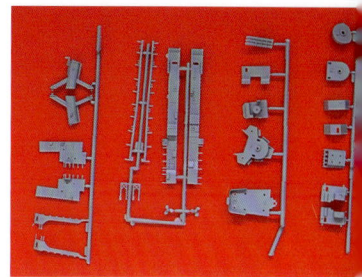

NEPTUNIA – UK   1:200 Scale

This cardboard model of the Canadian 'River' class frigate HMCS *Waskesiu* (CF003) is printed in a 30-page, A4 size book. To assist the construction, Neptunia can also supply three A4 sheets of laser cut frames, a sheet of etched brass, a set of brass rod for the masts, booms and flag staffs, and a set of brass weapons.

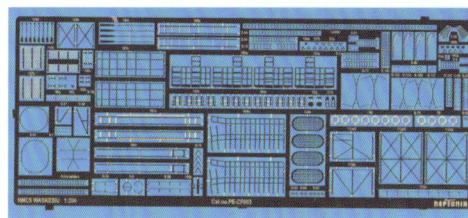

This is a full-hull model and the instructions include a page of technical information, a page of written instructions and eight pages of assembly diagrams. In the centre is a double page profile and plan drawing with an isometric drawing on the reverse. The frames are drawn on thin paper as they need to be stuck to card if not using the optional laser cut parts. The other parts are colour printed on card, ready to be cut out and assembled. There is also a page of templates, mainly for parts that need to be formed of wire.

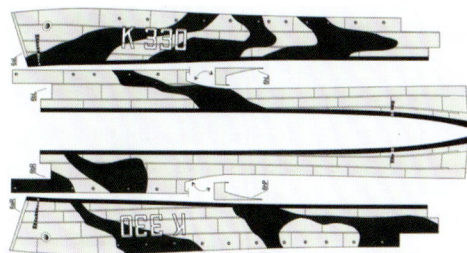

The etched brass sheet includes parts such as depth charge rails and stowages, bottoms of the Carley floats, supports for the AA gun platform and oars for the boats, but no guardrails. The set of brass rod for the masts, etc are all pre-cut to length and the set of barrels includes two 4in and four 20mm barrels, together with twenty-four projectiles for the Hedgehog mortar.

This model is well thought-out and will be greatly enhanced by the addition of the etched brass sheet and the brass weapons.

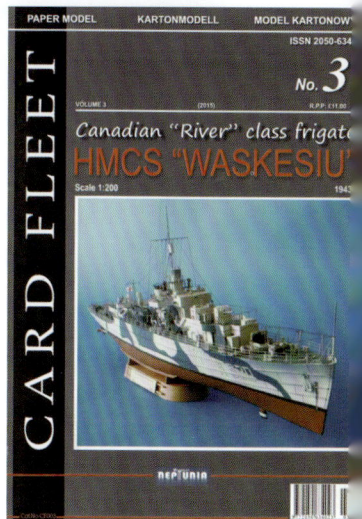

WAK – POLAND   1:200 Scale

This card model of the destroyer escort USS *England* is contained in an A4 size book, with historical and technical details of the vessel inside the front cover, together with assembly instructions. Inside the back cover is a general arrangement drawing showing the locations of the various assemblies shown elsewhere. The stand for the full-hull model is on the back, which will, of course, interrupt this drawing when cut-out.

Assembly diagrams are contained on four pages and there is a sheet of black and white photographs of the model. The basic hull parts are contained on two sheets which need to be attached to thicker card for use. There are six pages of card with all the parts printed in full colour. As these are single-sided some parts are duplicated as mirror images so that they can be stuck back-to-back where they are visible from both sides.

Parts such as depth charge rails are provided in card and these fine parts will require very careful cutting out and assembly if they are to appear realistic.

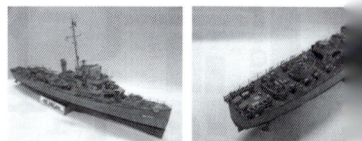

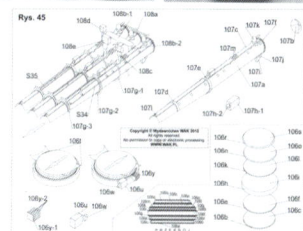

DEANES MARINE – UK

1:96 Scale

■ This manufacturer offers a range of kits for radio control operation, including HM Ships *Amethyst*, *Loch Katrine*, *Morecambe Bay* and *Tintagel Castle*. Future releases will include HMS *Enchantress*, the *Bittern* class sloop which served as an Admiralty yacht, and a 'River' class frigate.

The kits are all of a similar format with a grp hull, plastic card decks and superstructure, vacform mouldings for parts such as the funnel and boats, etched brass stanchions and mast and lengths of balsa and ramin wood. There is a comprehensive set of instructions and a DVD containing numerous helpful photographs of a model under construction.

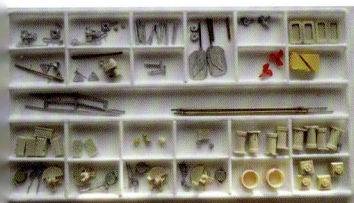

A range of fittings are supplied in a mixture of plastic, white metal and resin, all of which are clearly labelled in plastic trays.

ACCESSORIES

TOM'S MODELWORKS – USA

1:700 Scale

■ The small etched brass sheet #713 measures just 9.5cm x 3.5cm and is designed for use with a number of different 1:700 scale models of US destroyer escorts. The single double-sided sheet of instructions begins with some advice on handling and cleaning the sheet and then goes on to point out that some differences do exist between the different kits and that research is required to identify the specific fit of the subject to be modelled.

The first area covered is the mast and the SA radar antenna. Next the ladders and the figures (22 are included) are addressed. This is followed by details of the depth charge racks and stowages before moving on to the single 20mm gun mounts. Next is the anchor chain and guardrails – the instructions do point out that some vessels had netting on the rails and that this is available as set #714.

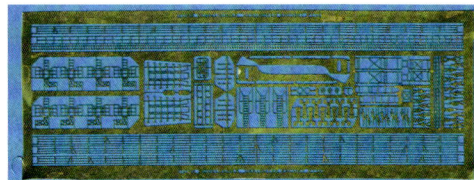

The spray shields along the superstructure sides are then fitted together with the various supports for the raised gun tubs. Similar frames are supplied for the life rafts. The last point is the optional mainmast, which is not supplied, with the HF/DF antenna.

A useful and flexible sheet.

TOM'S MODELWORKS – USA

1:350 Scale

■ This latest sheet of etched brass #3558 from Tom's Modelworks for *Buckley* class destroyer escorts varies in a number of ways from previous releases provided as stand-alone items, or as part of an Iron Shipwright resin kit at the same scale. There are two sheets: the larger sheet measures 15cm x 9.5cm and the smaller sheet just 8cm x 4cm and they are intended primarily for use with the Trumpeter kit of the USS *England*. The two double-sided sheets of instructions begin with some advice on handling and cleaning the sheet, before going on to point out that some differences do exist between different vessels, hence the inclusion of different types of handrails – 2- and 3-bar with separate netting and 2-bar combined with the netting.

Two sets of life raft netting are provided on each sheet, although the instructions only refer to two kit parts, C5 and C11. The flotation baskets provided are in a different form to previously and now include semicircular ends. The depth charge racks are referred to as being suitable for 'Late War Mark 9 Depth Charges', and once again differ from those supplied previously, as do the loading racks.

A total of four Stokes Litters, with separate wood slats, are provided, together with 10 shields and details for the 20mm guns. Kit part A2 is replaced with a fine antenna for the SA radar and other antennas for other sensors are also provided. The normal ladders, gun depression rails and life raft supports are provided but one noticeable addition is the details for the boat, including the pulleys located between the davits.

The main contents of the smaller sheet is flooring for the 3in gun tubs and details for the 3in guns. Some interesting additions but photographic references are needed to confirm exactly where and when the items were fitted.

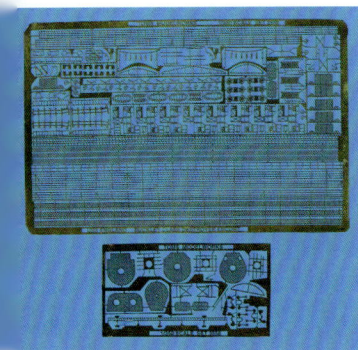

WHITE ENSIGN MODELS – UK   1:350 Scale

■ The PE3594 sheet of etched brass measures 21cm x 13cm and is designed for use with the Trumpeter kit of USS *England*. It can be used to enhance the basic kit or, with some additional resin parts, to modify the kit to represent a typical 'Captain' class frigate. The additional resin parts required are a 25ft motor boat, a 27ft whaler and eight RN pattern Carley rafts. Previously, these were available from WEM but suitable items can now be obtained from Black Cat Models (France) or Admiralty Model Works (USA).

For the US *Buckley* class, details are provided for the 3in gun mountings and replacement etched brass mountings for the single 20mm mountings and the quad 1.1in AA mounting, although many modellers will prefer to use resin replacement parts with more depth. Racks are provided for the depth charge arrangements and details for the Hedgehog mortar, Mark 51 Director and lookout sights. A replacement SP radar antenna is provided with additional mast details. Replacement spray shields are provided for use on the forward superstructure as are details for the funnel, the bridge and depression rails for both forward and aft gun mountings. Railings

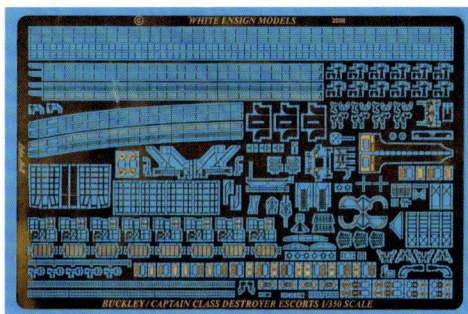

are provided for the full length of the ship, together with accommodation ladders, doors and hatches, which can be displayed open or closed.

Modifications required to represent a 'Captain' class vessel include shields for the 3in guns, with flare launchers for 'B' mounting, an etched brass 2pdr bow chaser if fitted, a different depth charge arrangement, mast details, with alternative HF/DF and Type 291 radar antennas, whaler davits and racks for the Carley rafts.

Various notes point out that there were many outfit variations for these vessels and so detailed research is required to accurately model any specific vessel at a specific time.

BLACK CAT MODELS – FRANCE   1:350 Scale

■ This is a new company who produce a range of accessories using 3D printing

techniques. Those applicable include the 27ft whaler, the 25ft motor boat, the Hedgehog anti-submarine mortar, Carley floats, 3in/50 Mark 22 gun, Mark 2 and Mark 4 depth charge throwers, 1.1in/75 quad gun mount, Mark 51 director, depth charge rails and floater net baskets.

The range available increases regularly and all items are both accurate and detailed.

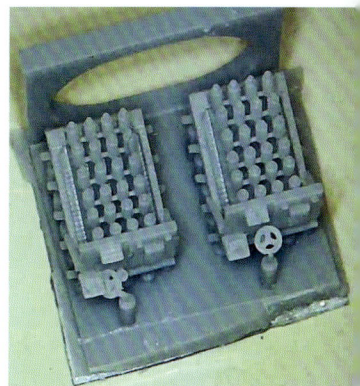

VETERAN MODELS – TAIWAN   1:350 Scale

■ Veteran Models produce a wide range of accessories including a very detailed model of the quad 1.1in gun mounting plus its Mark 44 director. Each mounting comprises four resin components, four brass barrels and a number of etched brass details, including the operators' seats. Each director comprises two resin components and some etched brass details, again including seats. Instructions are very clear and there are four mountings in a pack.

INFINI MODEL – REPUBLIC OF KOREA   1:350 Scale

■ Infini Model produce a number of accessories made entirely in brass. The Vickers 0.5in quad mount, of which there are six in a pack, comprises a milled brass central column, four turned barrels and some etched brass parts. The Mark IV

Oerlikon 20mm mounting is available as Royal Navy, USN rectangular or USN chamfered variants and there are twenty-five in a pack. These are very detailed but do come with clear instructions.

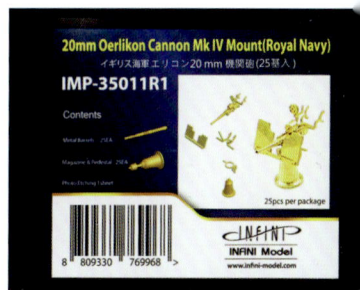

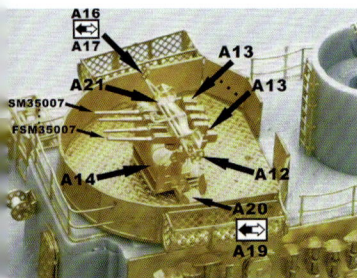

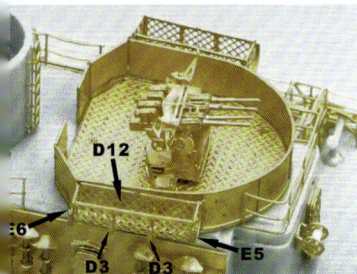

FIVE STAR DETAIL SET – CHINA

1:350 Scale

■ This is a magnificent set for use with the Trumpeter kit of USS *England* and consists of six sheets of etched brass, six resin parts (including a boat) and 28 brass parts (including barrels for the 3in, 20mm and 1.1in guns). The majority of etched brass is to cover the sides of the super-structure and gun tubs, with decking for the gun positions also. The high level of detail included is shown by the instruction photographs of the quad 1.1in mounting.

There are six pages of instructions, the first identifying the parts included and the others containing colour photographs of the various assemblies – bow, bridge & funnel, midships and aft. The last page contains

two photographs of an overall model. In all these photographs, the etched brass is unpainted and so its colour shows up clearly against the grey of the plastic.

This is a detail set for the dedicated modeller!

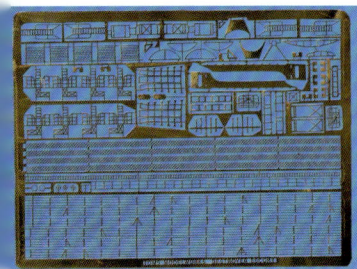

TOM'S MODELWORKS – USA

1:250 Scale

■ The etched brass sheet #250-01 measures 19cm x 14cm and is designed for use with the Revell 1:250 scale model of the *Buckley* class destroyer escort. The single double-sided sheet of instructions begins with some advice on handling and cleaning the sheet and then goes on to list ten references to part numbers within the kit where parts either need to be replaced by the etched brass or modified and then used in conjunction with the etched brass.

The first area covered is that of ladders and railings, both inclined and vertical ladders being included. Both 2- and 3-bar railings are supplied, plus rail netting for use where appropriate, depending on the particular vessel being modelled. Next comes the spray shields on the side of the superstructure, referred to as 'Side Wash Rail'.

Shields are supplied for ten 20mm gun mounts, scattered across the sheet, plus assemblies for the depth charge rails and stowages. Five floater net stowages are provided with a range of life raft supports.

Again, the instructions recommend checking references for the locations and styles required. Propeller guards are provided for use on both hull sides at the aft end.

A typical arrangement of the mainmast electronics, including the SA radar antenna, is given. The last point is the optional mainmast, which is not supplied, with the HF/DF antenna.

On the second side of the sheet, there is a plan and profile drawing showing the locations of the various parts. Options for the pipe-rails that physically limited the firing arcs of the guns are also shown in these drawings but no details are supplied as to which ones should be used, together with the blast shields and supporting brackets on both the forward and aft super-structure, the latter replacing the moulded parts supplied in the kit.

This sheet is dedicated to an old kit and will make a significant difference to the finished model, but more work is required to produce a truly accurate model from the Revell kit.

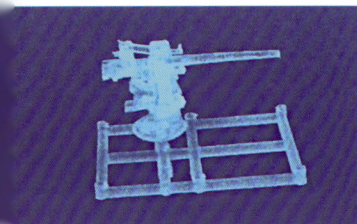

DI-STEFAN 3D PRINT – SERBIA

1:250 Scale

■ Di-Stefan produce a limited range of 1:250 scale accessories including the USN 3in/50 deck gun. This highly detailed gun will enhance the Revell kit of HMS *Bligh*. Di-Stefan also produce a set

comprising a single 20mm Oerlikon gun and twin and quadruple 40mm guns, and some USN chocks (fairleads) which could also be of use. [available from shape-ways.com]

GOLD MEDAL MODELS *BUCKLEY/WARD* FITTING SET – USA

1:240 Scale

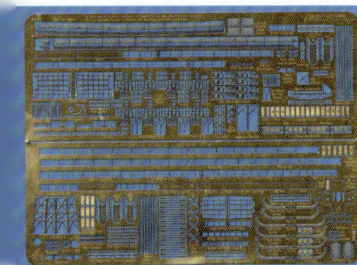

■ This set of etched brass is intended for use with both the Revell *Buckley* class destroyer escort and the *Ward* class destroyer. The sheet is of thick material and contains sufficient parts to complete one model of each type. The instructions are supplied on a single, large double-sided sheet and show the various assemblies in

individual windows, each of which identifies which of the two types of vessels they are applicable to. On the second side, a profile drawing assists the modeller to identify the locations of the assemblies. These include details for the guns and depth charges, a radar antenna and mast details, and details for the boats and life rafts.

Modelmakers' Showcase

ATLANTIC MODELS *AMETHYST* 1:350 scale

By CHRIS HEWITT

This ship became famous when, on 20 April 1949, commanded by Lieutenant Commander Skinner, she became the captive of Chinese communist forces whilst sailing from Shanghai to Nanking along the River Yangtze. Her subsequent escape demonstrated clearly the fortitude and bravery of her crew. The colour of the water is typical of that of the Yangtze.

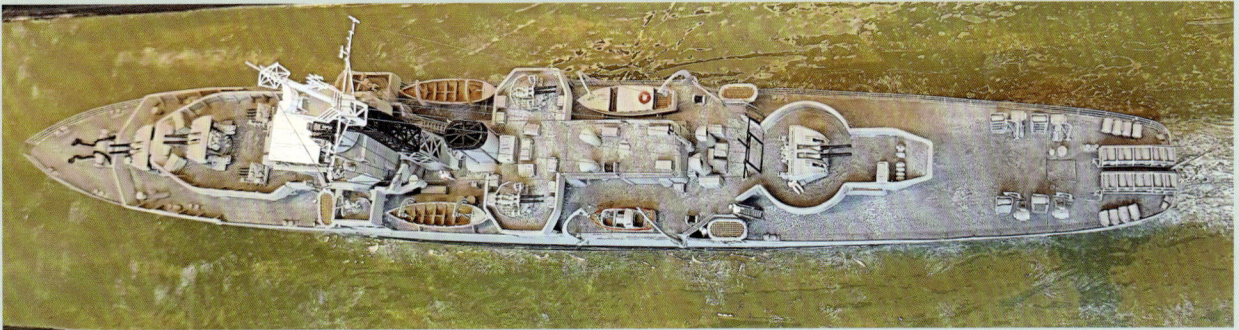

SCRATCH-BUILT *AMETHYST* 1:72 scale By JOHN EDWARDS

This working model represents HMS *Amethyst* at the time of the Korean War.

ATLANTIC MODELS *KITE* 1:350 scale By ROGER TORGESON

This model was based on the (as then) White Ensign Models kit of HMS *Starling*. She is painted in white and WA blue.

The only extra items added to the build were a few vertical ladders and a small spreader bar to the lantern radar mast for the aerials running from the foremast. The cast-on resin cable reels located on the forward and aft superstructure parts were removed and replaced with a combination of round plastic stock and PE reel ends. In order to make the finished model a little different and unique Roger did replace the two cast white metal twin 40mm Bofors with WEM quad pom-poms, the cast metal barrels on the 4in HA/LA mounts with brass replacements and the PE 20mm with modified Tamiya plastic parts.

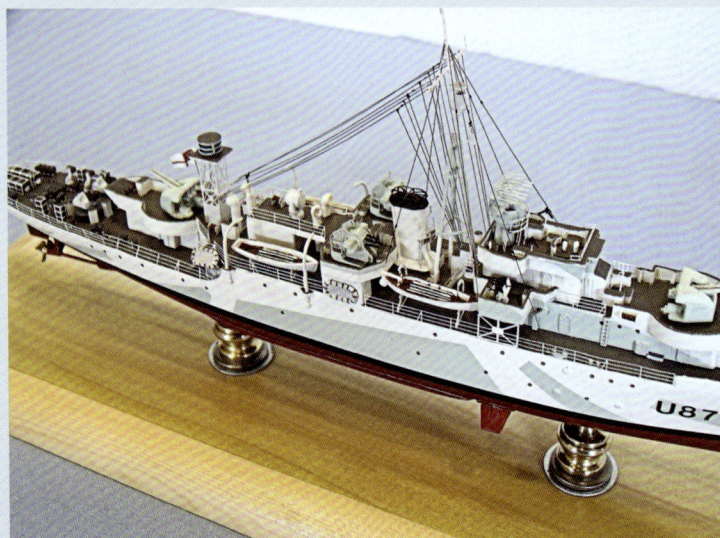

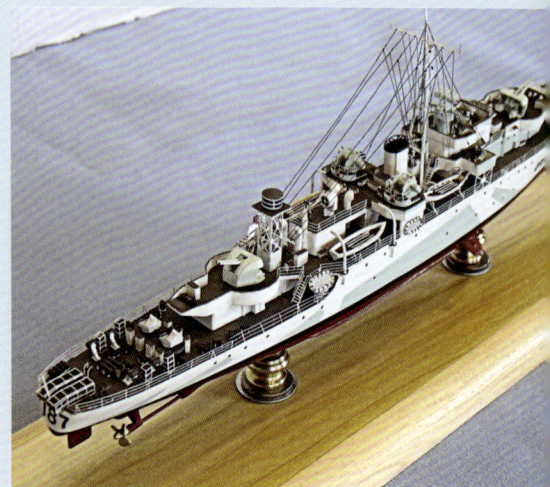

AJM MODELS *BLACK SWAN* AND *IBIS* 1:700 scale By DAVE EYLES

These two models from Poland are built 'straight from the box' and depict *Black Swan* in her pre-war grey and *Ibis* in a complicated five-coloured camouflage scheme including MS4A (very light grey), MS4 (mid grey), B6 (mid blue grey), B5 (dark blue grey) and MS1 (grey black) with some black 'outlining'. Both decks are unpainted wood (teak).

ATLANTIC MODELS *STARLING* 1:350 scale   By IAN RUSCOE

In this model, Ian wanted to represent HMS *Starling* in typical sea conditions for many of her operations. As the kit is water-line and parts of the bottom show as the vessel moves, it was important to include an underwater hull section.

ATLANTIC MODELS *STARLING* 1:350 scale   By PETE STERN

This model does not carry the compli-cated camouflage pattern of that built by Ian Ruscoe, and the sloop is displayed in much calmer waters but Pete has carried out some severe 'weathering' on his model, typical of these hard-working vessels.

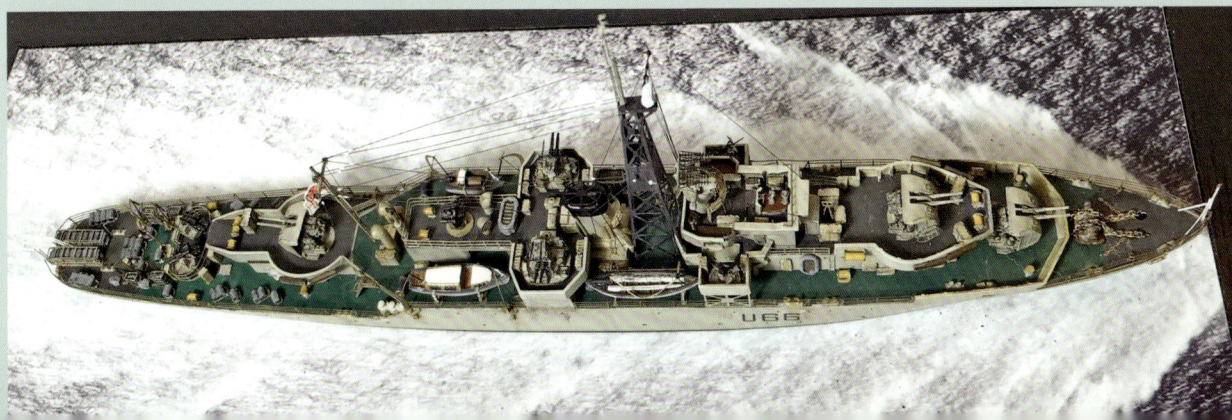

SCRATCH-BUILT *WILD GOOSE* (c1943) 1:96 scale By DAVID McNAIR TAYLOR

The model is scratch-built based on a second-hand Deans Marine *Amethyst* hull. A lot of research was required to modify it to the 1943 layout, which is considerably different from the post-war *Amethyst*. David used John Lambert's plan for *Starling*, the superstructure being scratch-built with plasticard etc. Some of the fittings David moulded in resin and some were purchased from John Haynes and Scalewarship. In addition, a few of the Deans Marine kit fittings were used. The camouflage and general layout of the ship was taken from photographs and other online and book research.

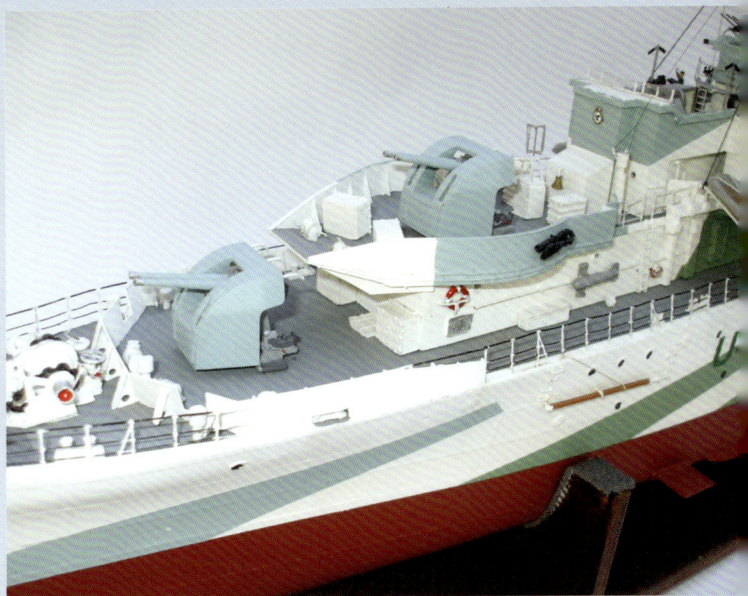

ATLANTIC MODELS *SHEARWATER* 1:350 scale By FELIX BUSTELO

This model was built using the White Ensign Models kit of HMS *Kittiwake* and displays a white hull with the lower part of the hull in WA green, similar to that worn by *Kittiwake*, but with no pennant number. Note the splinter matting around the forward gun. The flying boat, with its attendant launch, adds great interest to the completed model.

STARLING MODELS *NADDER* 1:350 scale   By DAVE EYLES

This 'River' class frigate is another model built 'straight from the box' but with the high level of detail included in this kit, very few enhancements or additions need to be made.

ATLANTIC MODELS *KITTIWAKE* 1:350 scale By PETE STERN

This model, originally from White Ensign Models, clearly shows the lower profile of the *Kingfisher* class sloops with her 4in gun on the forecastle and a quad 0.5in mounting on the quarterdeck. Note the high number of depth charge throwers carried.

ATLANTIC MODELS *GORLESTON* 1:350 scale

By DAVE EYLES

The very different appearance of the ex-USCG cutters from the other escorts is immediately obvious in this model which was built 'straight from the box' but with the guns replaced by 3D printed parts from Black Cat Models.

TRUMPETER *BICKERTON* 1:350 scale By PHIL REEDER

This model was built from the Trumpeter USS *England* kit, using the White Ensign Models etched brass set to convert the outfit to that of a 'Captain' class frigate. The boats are 3D printed parts from Black Cat Models and the camouflage pattern was the result of Phil's diligent research.

ATLANTIC MODELS *PORTCHESTER CASTLE* 1:350 scale By IAN RUSCOE

This diorama of the vessel alongside with dockside buildings and a small auxiliary vessel passing is very atmospheric and displays this fine model of a 'Castle' class escort to great advantage.

Note that because of the great number and variety of escorts it is not always possible to attribute a specific scheme to an individual ship at a particular time; therefore, many of the schemes that follow are representative only. *(All drawings by George Richardson)*

HMS *Enchantress*
Bittern class sloop as Admiralty Yacht, 1935

WHITE

BUFF

BLACK

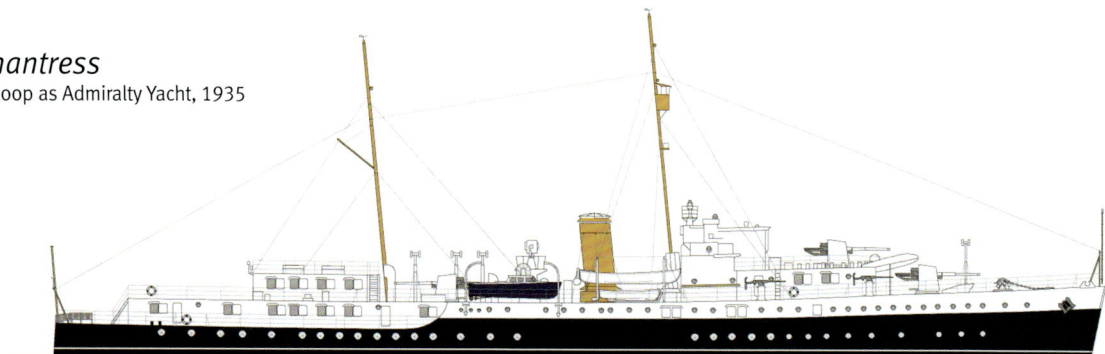

HMAS *Yarra*
Australian *Grimsby* class sloop, 1940.
An unofficial scheme

507B   507C

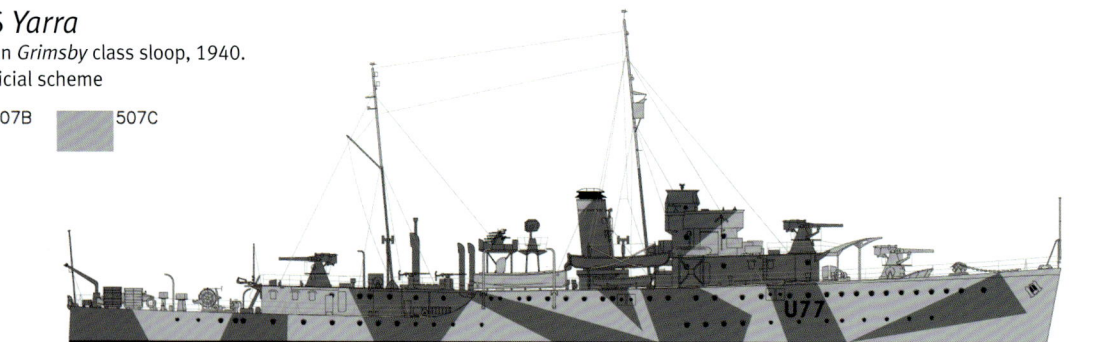

HMS *Kittiwake*
Kingfisher class sloop. As at beginning of war, 1939

507A

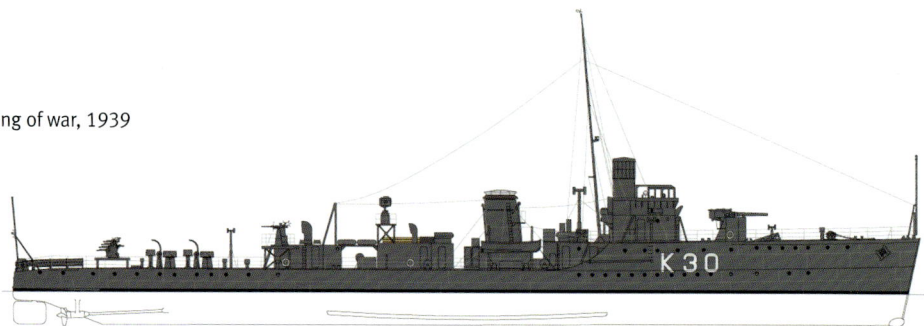

HMS *Kittiwake*
Kingfisher class sloop. Western Approaches type, 1942

WESTERN APPROACHES
BLUE (1941)

WESTERN APPROACHES
GREEN (1941)

WHITE

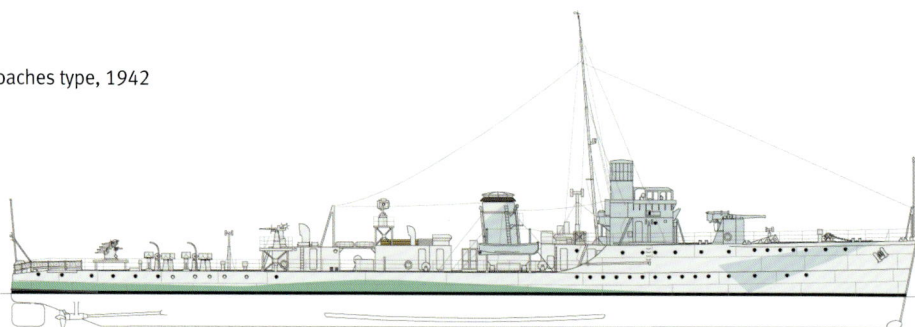

Egret class sloops
Dark Admiralty type

507A (1940)

MS 3   MS 4 (1941)

Egret class sloops
Western Approaches type, 1942

WESTERN APPROACHES
BLUE (1941)

WESTERN APPROACHES
GREEN (1941)

WHITE

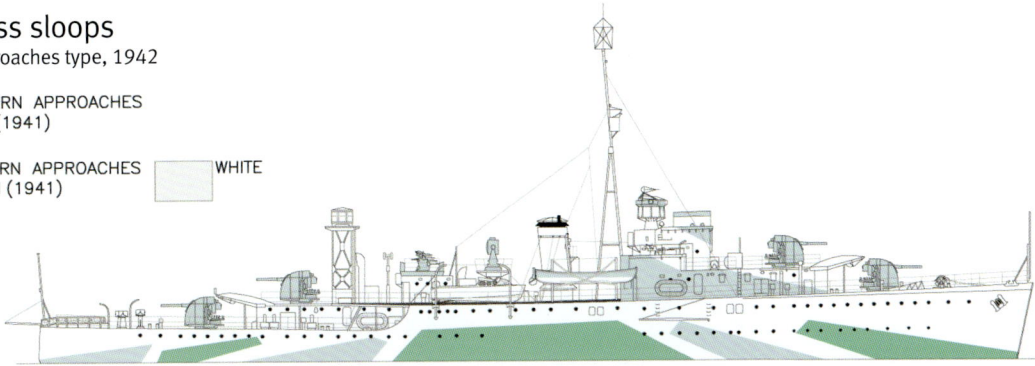

Egret class sloops
Western Approaches type, 1943

WESTERN APPROACHES
BLUE (1941)

WHITE

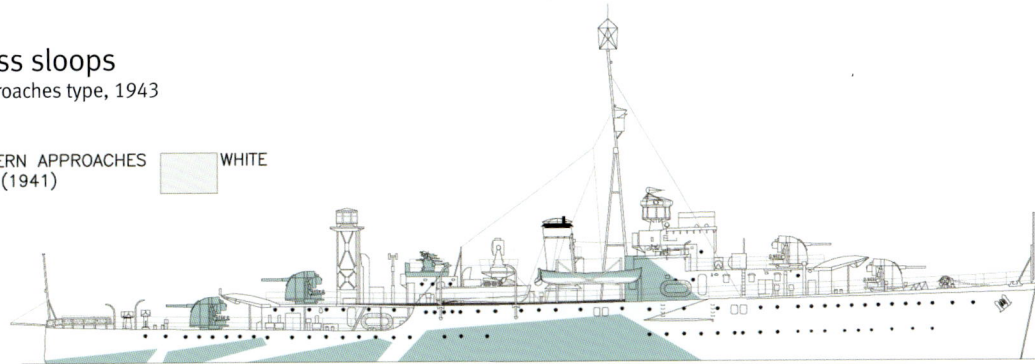

HMS *Black Swan*
Black Swan class sloop, February 1942

WESTERN APPROACHES
BLUE (1941)

WHITE

(Boot topping not painted over)

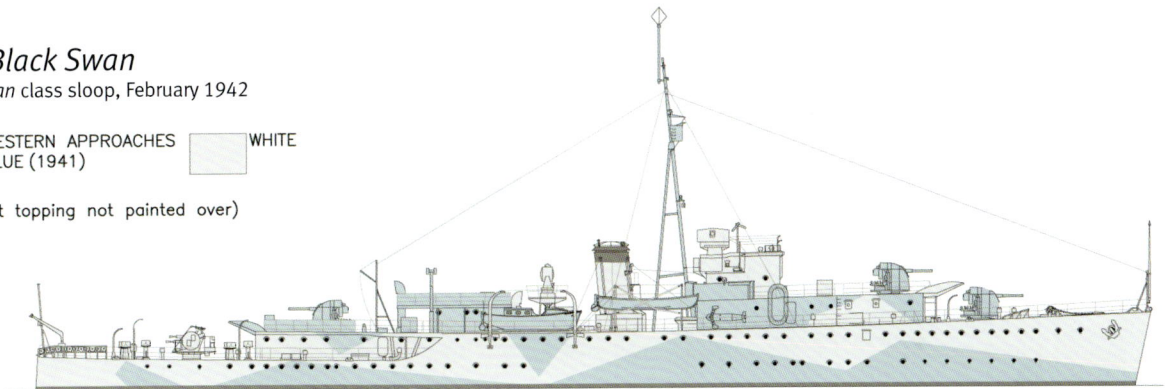

Modified *Black Swan* class sloops
Western Approaches type, 1942

WESTERN APPROACHES
BLUE (1941)

WESTERN APPROACHES
GREEN (1941)

WHITE

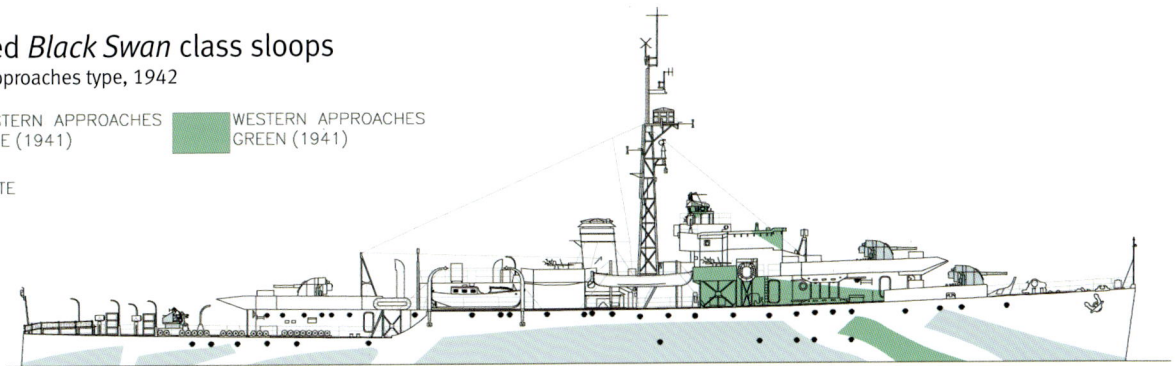

HMS *Starling*
Modified Black Swan class sloop.
Light Admiralty type, 1943

MS 1   MS 3

'River' class frigates
Early war schemes – Western Approaches type, 1942

WESTERN APPROACHES
BLUE (1941)　　　　WHITE

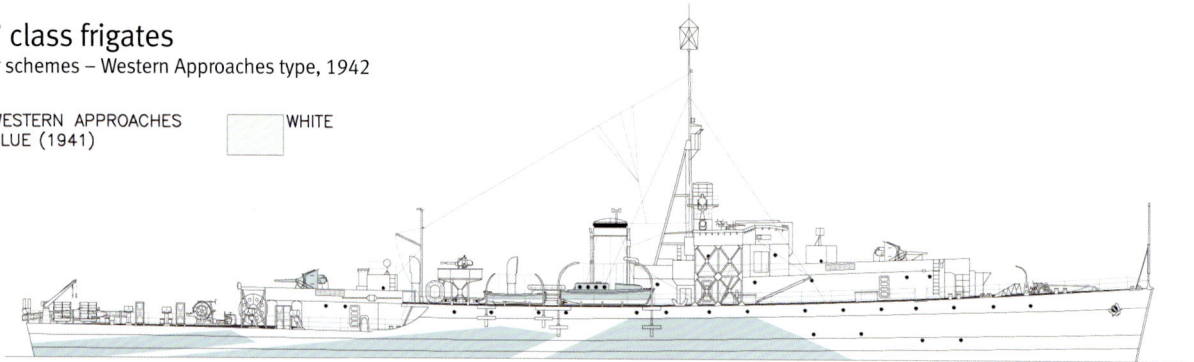

'River' class frigates
Early war schemes – Light Admiralty type

G 10　　B 30　　G 45　　B 55

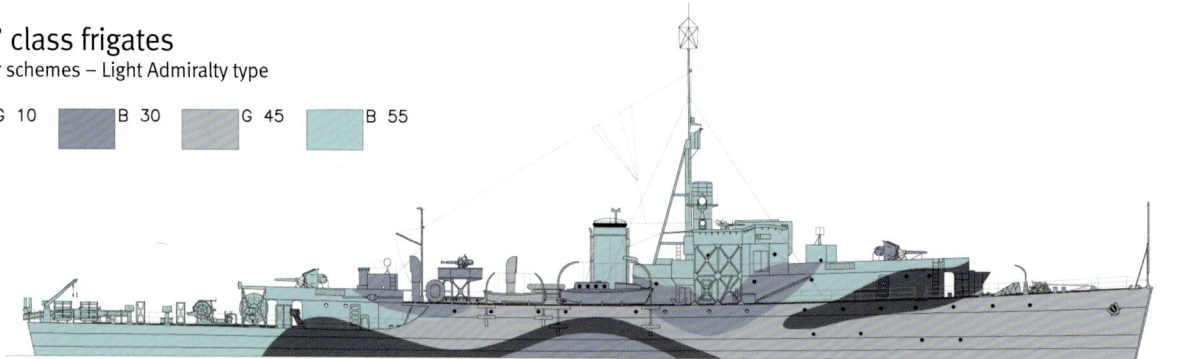

'River' class frigates
Early war schemes – Intermediate type

G 10　　G 20　　G 45

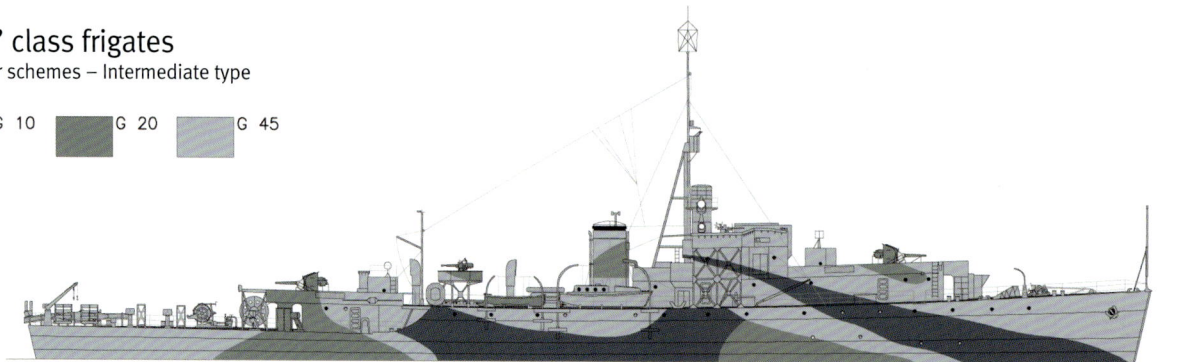

'River' class frigates
Late war – Admiralty Standard Scheme 'D'

G 45　　B 55

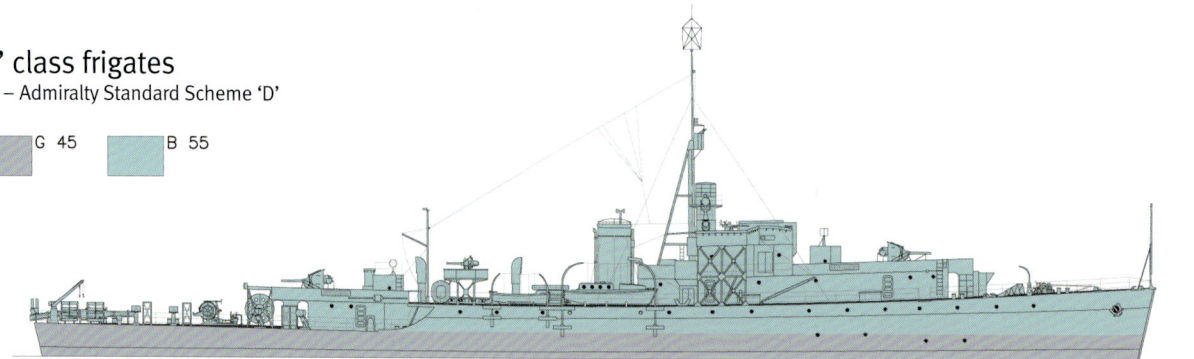

'River' class frigates
Late war – Admiralty Standard Scheme 'C'

WHITE　　B 55

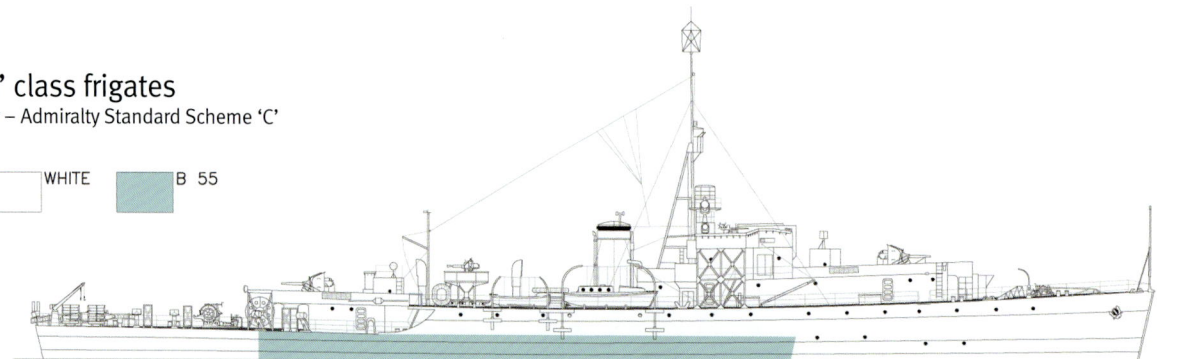

HMS *Portchester Castle*
'Castle' class frigate,1943

WESTERN APPROACHES
BLUE (1941)

WHITE

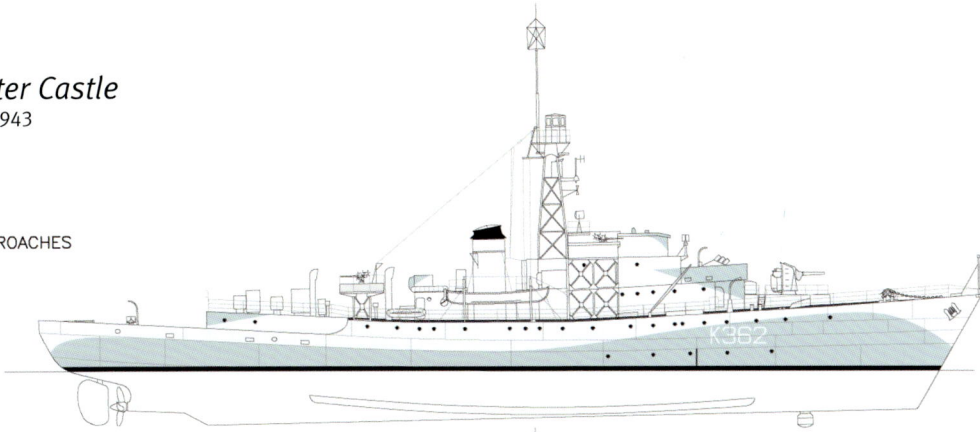

HMS *Brougham Castle*
'Castle' class frigate,1944

WESTERN APPROACHES
BLUE (1941)

WHITE

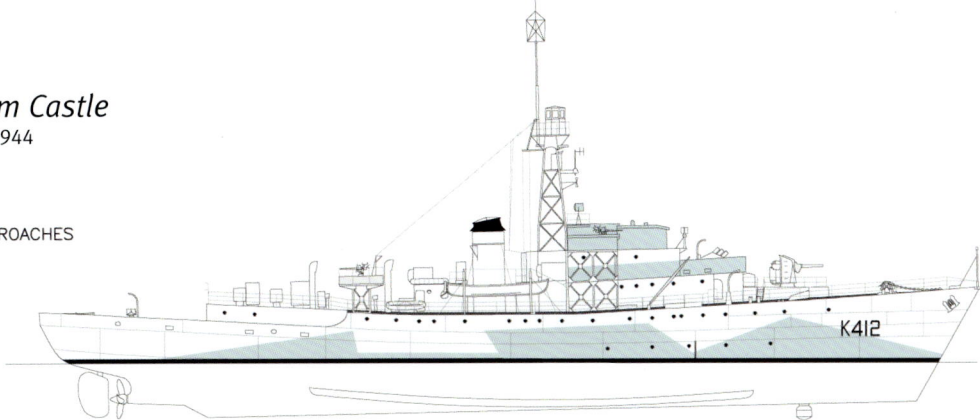

Ex-US *Evarts* type
RN 'Captain' class – delivery colours

PALE GRAY
5–P

SEA BLUE
5–S

Ex-US *Evarts* type
RN 'Captain' class – Admiralty Type 'D'

B 55

G 45

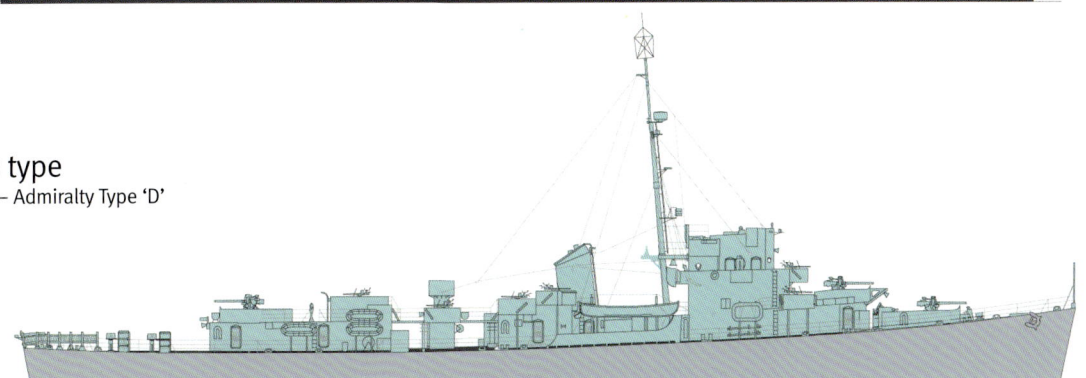

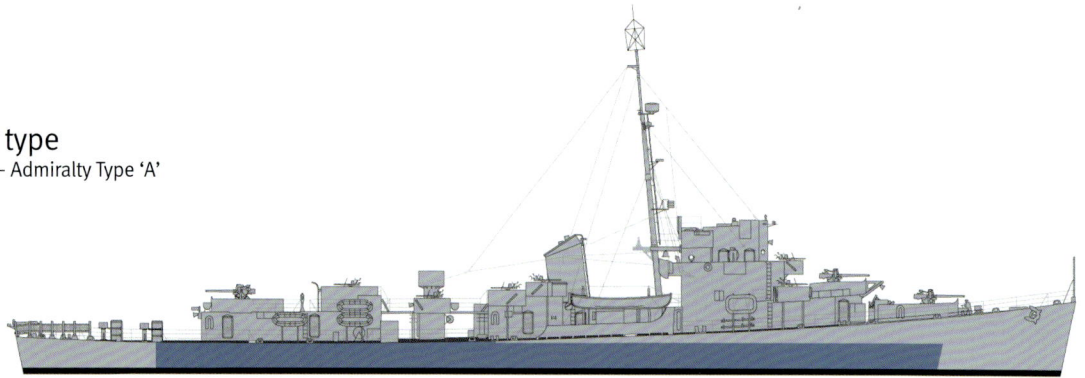

Ex-US *Evarts* type
RN 'Captain' class – Admiralty Type 'A'

B 20
G 45

Ex-US *Evarts* type
RN 'Captain' class – Admiralty Intermediate Type

G 10
B 15
G 45

Ex-US *Evarts* type
RN 'Captain' class – Light Admiralty Type

G 10
B 30
G 45
B 55

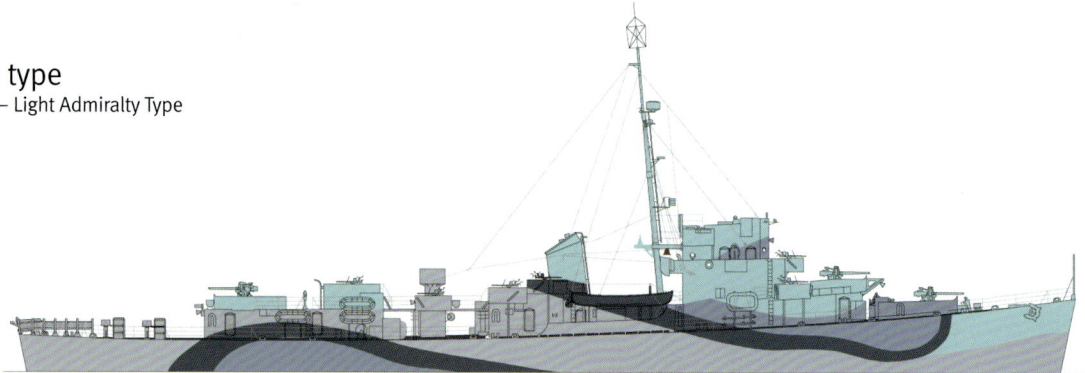

Ex-US *Evarts* type
RN 'Captain' class – Western Approaches type, 1943

WESTERN APPROACHES
BLUE(1941)

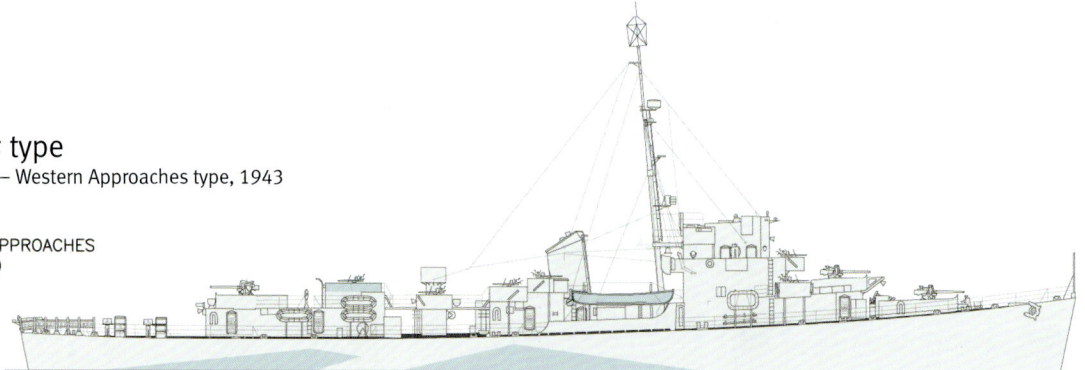

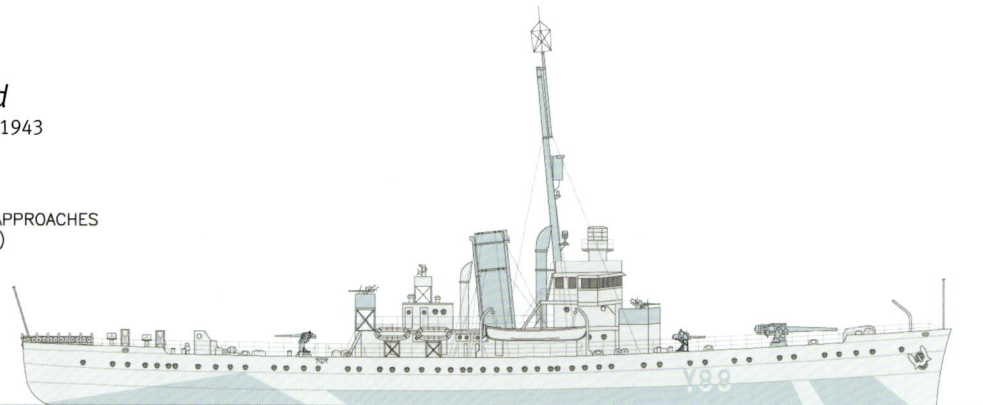

WHITE

HMS *Totland*
'Lake' class sloop,1943

WESTERN APPROACHES
BLUE(1941)

WHITE

CAMOUFLAGE

Sloops and frigates operated in many different theatres of war and the paint schemes worn by them were very varied. In the early part of the war, before the Admiralty issued official patterns and were using the resources available to design camouflage patterns for major warships, many of the Captains and/or their 1st Lieutenants designed unofficial patterns using whatever paint was available, usually that in the vessel's paint store or available from the port where they were based.

The sloops involved with escorting the North Atlantic convoys in the early 1940s, frequently had white hulls with areas of WA green and/or WA blue. In the following years, Admiralty schemes introduced a greater use of grey, blue and black and less use of green and white.

Enchantress, a member of the *Bittern* class, had been completed as an Admiralty yacht and before the war carried a 'Victorian livery' of black hull, white superstructure and ochre funnel. With the additional accommodation removed and some enhancement to her guns, in 1941 she had a B6 grey hull and 507C grey upperworks. In 1943, having received a Hedgehog mortar and additional depth charges, her hull had areas of green and blue added. As a Landing Ship (HQ), in 1945 the lower half of her hull was painted in PB10 over its entire length.

Some of the *Black Swan* class were painted with white hulls, with areas of green and blue, while others carried either the Admiralty Intermediate or Dark scheme with much greater emphasis on the use of grey. *Black Swan* was wearing a Pacific scheme at the end of the war – 507C light

Above: In this view of *Bridgewater* during the war, the aft polemast has been reduced in height, a HF/DF polemast added on the quarterdeck and the minesweeping davits have been removed. Note the radar system in a 'drum' on the bridge.

Left: *Scarborough* in August 1943 is very similar to *Bridgewater* in the wartime photograph above, having received similar modifications.

Right: The original Thornycroft design of depth charge thrower.

Below, left: The Hedgehog ahead throwing mortar on a 'River' class frigate. HMS *Spey* lies longside.

Below, right: The projectiles from a Hedgehog mortar land in the water ahead of the escort. The civilians on the bridge suggest trials of the weapon.

pattern was the 5-charge in which three DCs were released from the rail and two were projected abeam, to result in a diamond with a central point.

The first changes were put in hand to try to 'bracket' the target so that a change of depth in the last stage of the attack could be forestalled. By the installation of two rails and four throwers a double diamond (*ie*, one diamond superimposed on another) could be laid and one pair of throwers (the forward pair) and one rail (the port one) were supplied with the DC Mark VII Heavy. This was the standard charge with the addition of a cast iron weight of some 150lb to increase the sinking rate. At the same time,

new pistols were provided so that the standard Mark VII now had depth settings available of 50, 100, 150, 250, 350 and 500ft while the heavy charge had a pistol which gave 140, 225, 300, 385 and 500ft.

The next development was the fitting of another four throwers to allow a 14-charge pattern to be laid. This interposed a square of four charges on the double diamond of the 10-charge pattern, the four charges being between the two layers. There were standard settings laid down for the pistols – 5-charge patterns fired to either 50, 100 or 150ft; 14-charge patterns fired with the three layers at 100, 140 and 225ft; at 150, 225 and 300ft; or 250, 300 and 385ft.

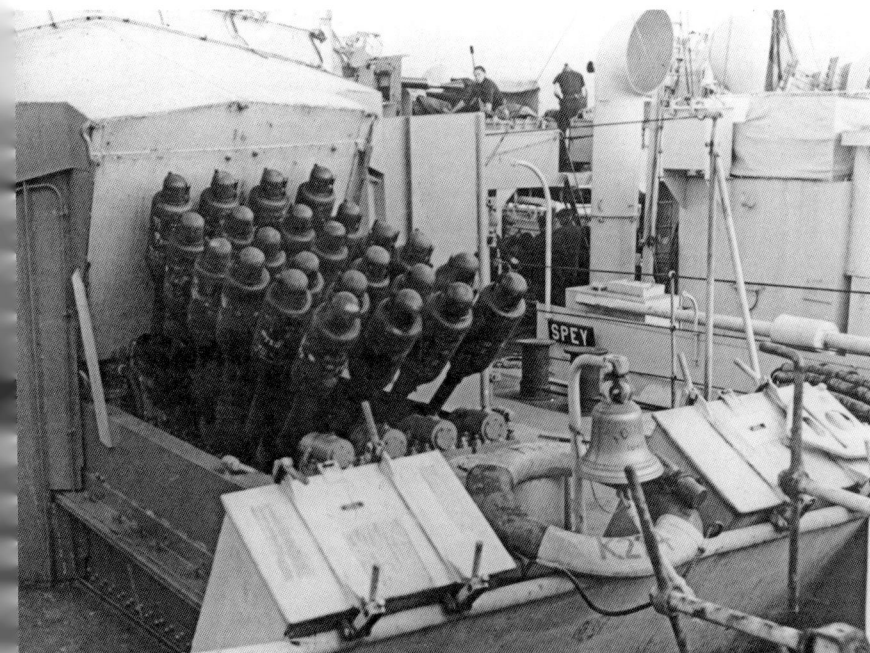

Left: HMS *Totland* wearing an interesting camouflage pattern.

The ten ex-USCG cutters of the *Banff* class were initially used to escort convoys between England and Sierra Leone, during which HMS *Culver* was hit by two torpedoes fired by *U-105* on 31 January 1942 and sank south-west of Ireland following a magazine explosion. The remaining cutters were assigned to Operation Torch where *Hartland* and *Walney* were both lost to gunfire. The remaining seven escorted Mediterranean convoys in support of the North African invasion and saw varied employment in the Atlantic until transferred to the Indian Ocean for the remainder of the war escorting trade convoys. Five served in the Bay of Bengal supporting Operation Dracula and Operation Zipper in the last months of conflict with Japan.

Despite their heavy involvement and attacking a number of both German and Japanese submarines, the cutters only sank two. *Sennen* was credited with sinking *U-954* while defending convoy SC130 on 19 May 1943. Among the crew of this U-boat was Peter Dönitz, the son of Admiral Karl Dönitz. *Totland* sank *U-522* on 23 February 1943 while escorting the tanker convoys UC1 and CU1.

Fifty-Nine 'River' class frigates were commissioned into the RN, eight of which had been built in Canada, and they sank one Italian and sixteen German submarines in 1943 and 1944. Three of these frigates, *Itchen*, *Mourne* and *Tweed*, were sunk by submarines during this same period and two more were torpedoed, becoming constructive total losses.

HMS *Jed* was assigned to the 1st Support Group, also including *Pelican*,

Below: This August 1943 photo of *Erne* clearly shows the layout of the *Black Swan* class sloops with two twin 4in guns forward and one aft, 20mm guns in the bridge wings and on a platform just aft of the funnel, a 3in AA gun on the superstructure forward of the lattice mast supporting the radar and a quadruple pom-pom on the quarterdeck.

Above: HMS *Tay* in August 1942 carries the usual camouflage pattern worn by many escorts operating in the North Atlantic.

Below: *Cygnet* appears to have recently received a new coat of camouflage paint. The quadruple pom-pom aft of the funnel can be clearly seen but note the retention of a crowsnest on the foremast with a radar on the lattice mast aft.

Above: A fine overhead photo of a 'Colony' class frigate, *Tortola* in August 1944, shows the simpler camouflage system used later in the war.

Sennen, Rother, Spey and *Wear*, on the 1st March 1943 and in April the support group formed part of the defence of convoy ONS5, together with the B7 Close Escort and the 3rd Support Group. This convoy suffered atrocious weather conditions and lost eleven merchant vessels but in return sank five German submarines.

The 'Colony' class did not really become involved in the battles in the North Atlantic or in British inshore waters but sank two German submarines in 1944 and four in 1945, without suffering any losses.

HMS *Ascension* became the senior officer's ship of the 17th Escort Group in September 1944 and in November the group were patrolling between the Shetland and Faroe Islands. A Sunderland flying boat reported a radar contact and the group sailed to investigate. *Ascension* gained asdic contact with *U-322* and attacked, together with *Moorsom*, using her Hedgehog with immediate success.

Approximately 50 of the 'Captain' class frigates were allocated at any one time to Western Approaches during 1944 and 1945. In the second half of 1944 and the first half of 1945, six Escort Groups of these frigates operated from Belfast. The 'Captain' class sank thirty-five German submarines at the cost of eight ex-*Buckley* and five ex-*Evarts* class vessels. Some of the class operated in support of coastal forces for which they were equipped with a 2pdr pom-pom 'bow-chaser' right forward as an anti-*schnellboot* measure.

HMS *Ekins* began her wartime career as a member of the 3rd Escort Group operating in the North Atlantic. She received a bow-chaser pom-pom upon joining the 21st Destroyer Flotilla in support of the Normandy landings. She spent D-day, and

Above: A fine overhead photo of a 'Colony' class frigate, *Tortola* in August 1944, shows the simpler camouflage system used later in the war.

Left: Note the 2pdr bow-chaser right forward in HMS *Ekins*.

Right: A Squid mortar.

Below: *Loch Morlich* carries the pennant number K517 painted in black on her camouflage scheme in this July 1944 view.

the days following, escorting convoys from the Thames to the Normandy beaches and back again. Whilst carrying out this task, she and *Curzon* sank the German submarine *U-212* off Brighton.

Six of the 'Castle' class were completed for the RN in late 1943, eighteen in 1944 and two in 1945. Twelve were also completed for the RCN and one for Norway. They escorted convoys in many different theatres and sank six German submarines, including *U-387* and *U-425* which were both sunk in the Barents Sea, east of the Rybachy Peninsula in December 1944 and February 1945,

respectively. A couple of months later, *U-878* was sunk in the Bay of Biscay. *Kenilworth Castle* was involved in the capture of *U-744* west of Ireland, after the submarine had been subjected to more than 30 hours of depth charging in March 1944. Unfortunately, the submarine had to be sunk when attempts to tow it failed.

The first submarine to be sunk by the Squid mortar was *U-736* on 6 August 1944. HMS *Loch Killin* fired her mortar and almost immediately a Gnat acoustic homing torpedo fired by the submarine exploded close to the frigate. *U-736* surfaced right under *Loch Killin*'s stern and

Left: *Porchester Castle* as completed in November 1943. The ship shows a number of the wartime improvements introduced into anti-submarine escorts, including a Squid mortar forward of the bridge, rocket flare launching rails on the 4in gun, and Type 272 radar in a 'lantern' atop the lattice mast.

14 survivors managed to scramble onto her quarterdeck before the submarine sank. The 'Loch' class sank sixteen German submarines, twelve of these in the first four months of 1945. None of the 'Lochs' were sunk during the war.

In April 1945 *Loch Insh* joined the escort for Russian Convoy JW66, arriving off Kola Inlet on the 25th. Four days later she carried out anti-submarine operations off the Inlet before departing with the return Convoy RA66. She sank *U-307* using Shark projectiles and Squid during the attacks. Shark projectiles could be fired by any 4in QF gun. It weighed 96½lbs, including a Torpex bursting charge of 24lbs. Overall length was 73½in of which 53½in was the body, the remainder being a finned tail.

There were two anti-ricochet nose rings and a base percussion fuse.

This weapon was intended to be fired such as to land 20yds short of the target submarine, striking the water at an entry angle of about 5° and then continue its trajectory underwater to the hull, where it was able to pierce any side tanks and detonate in contact with the pressure hull. Later the same day, other vessels in the Support Group sank *U-286*.

Loch Fyne was initially attached to the 18th Escort Group but, despite making attacks on a number of submarines, did not sink any. However, she did form part of the escort of ten surrendered submarines from Trondheim to Scapa Flow in May 1945, escorting nine to Loch Ryan in early June.

Below: A post-war aerial view of *Morecombe Bay* (in 1949) demonstrating the main features of the AA version of the 'Loch/Bay' design, principally the twin 4in mountings fore and aft, and a fire control system to accompany them (Type 293 radar at the masthead and a Mk VI rangefinder director on the bridge).

HMS *Amethyst*
Modified *Black Swan* class sloop, 1943

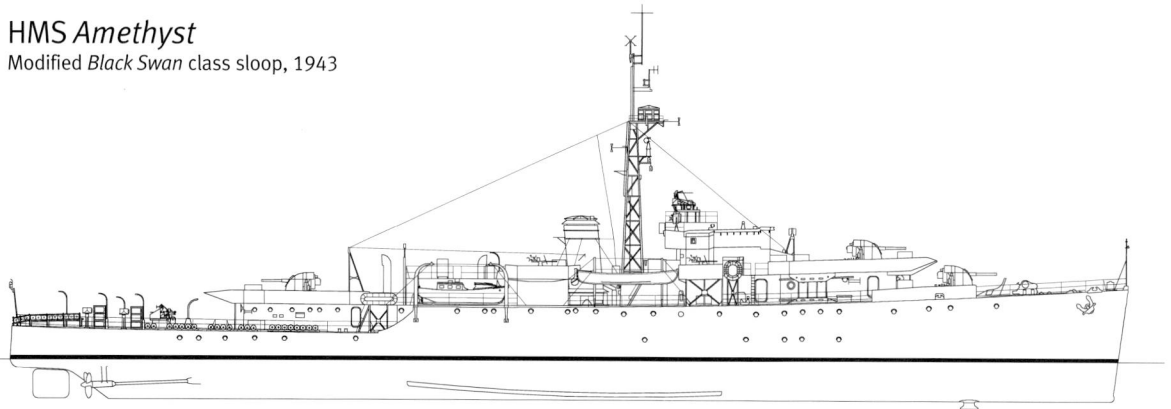

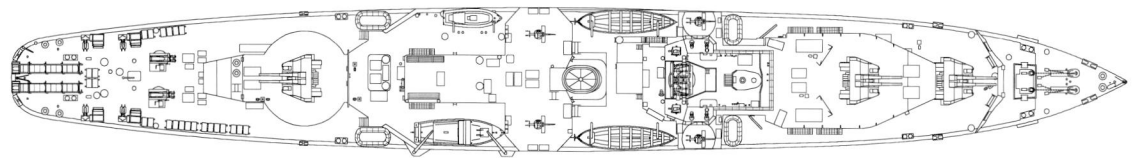

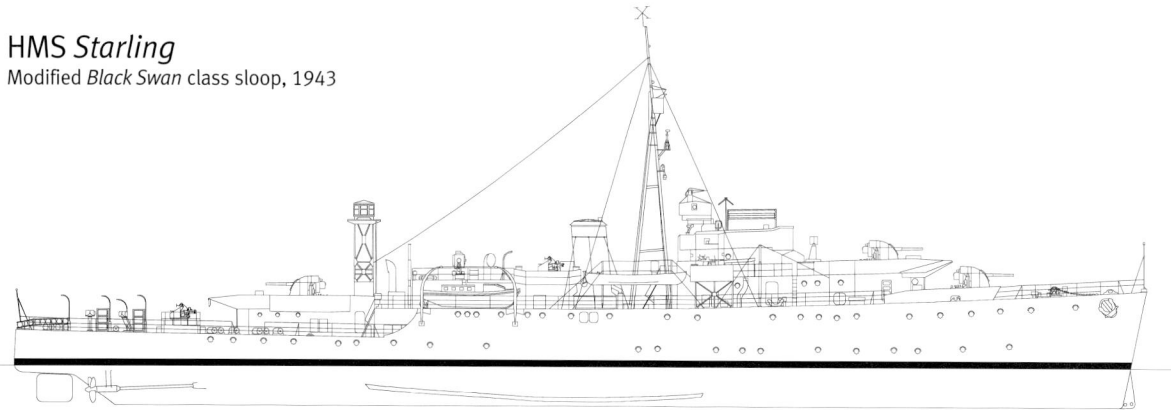

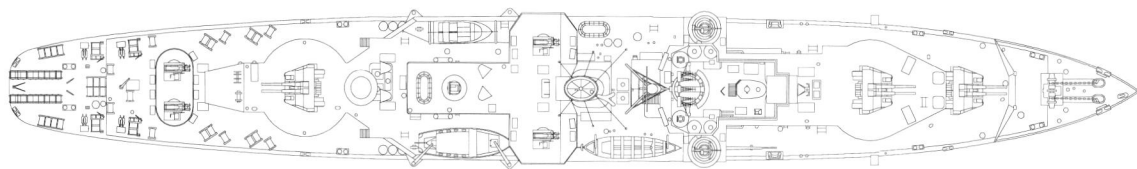

HMS *Starling*
Modified *Black Swan* class sloop, 1943

HMS *Spey*
'River' class frigate, 1942

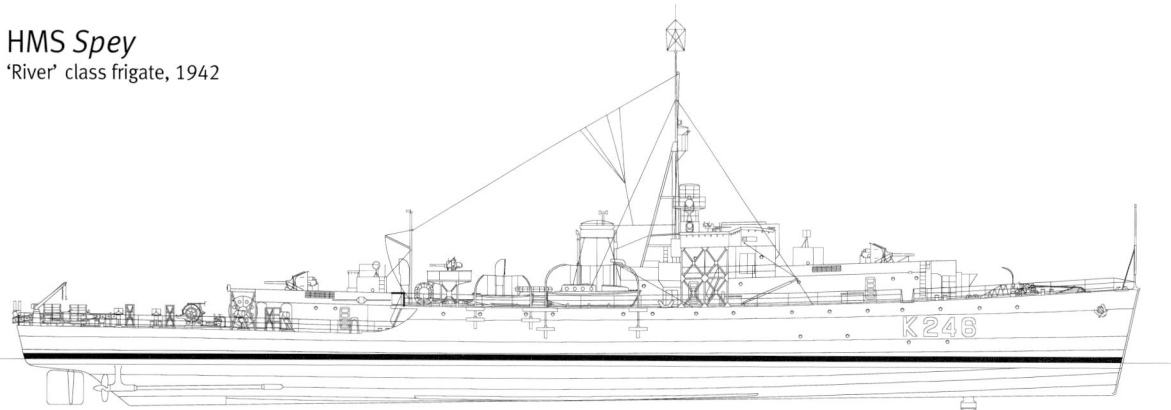

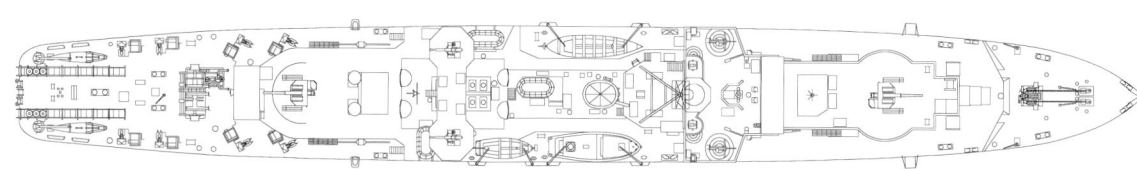

'Loch' class frigate
as completed

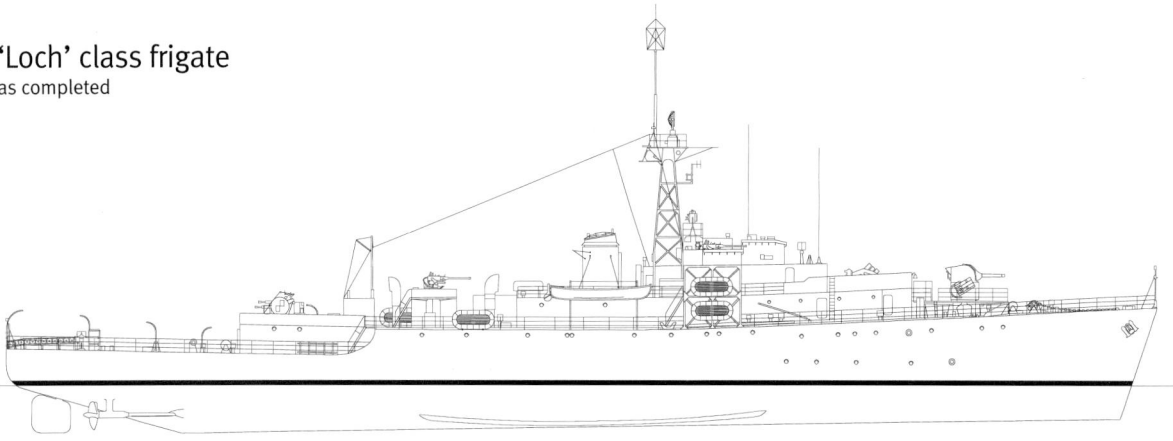

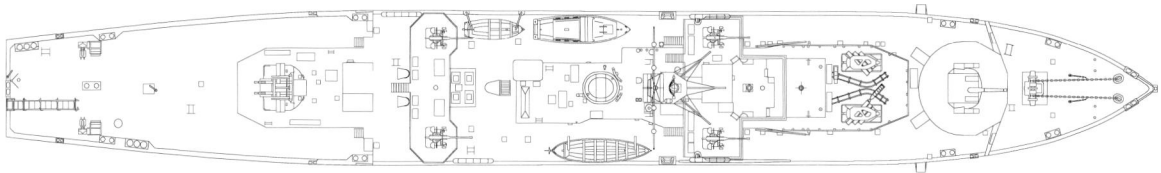

'Castle' class frigate
as completed

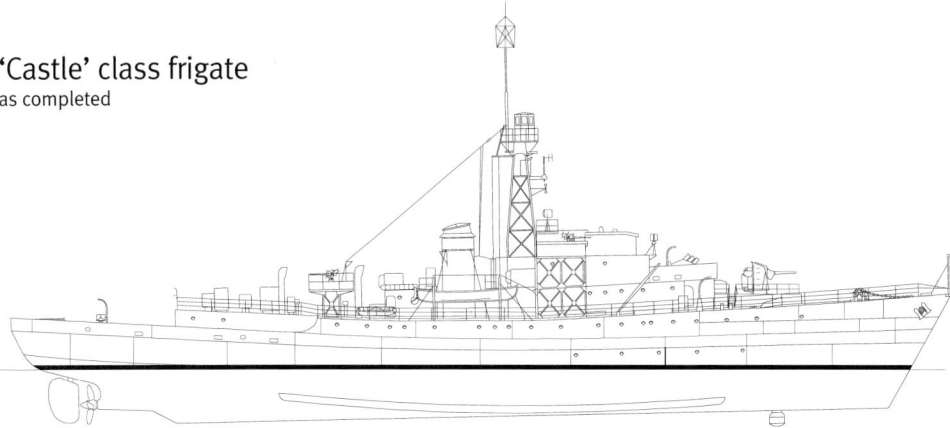

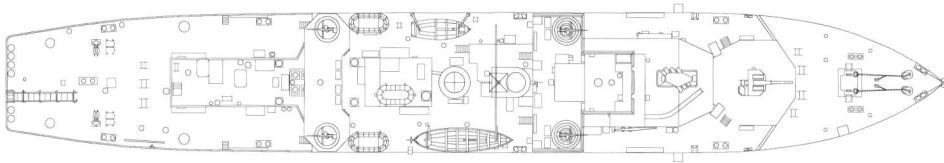

Australian 'Bay' class frigate
as completed

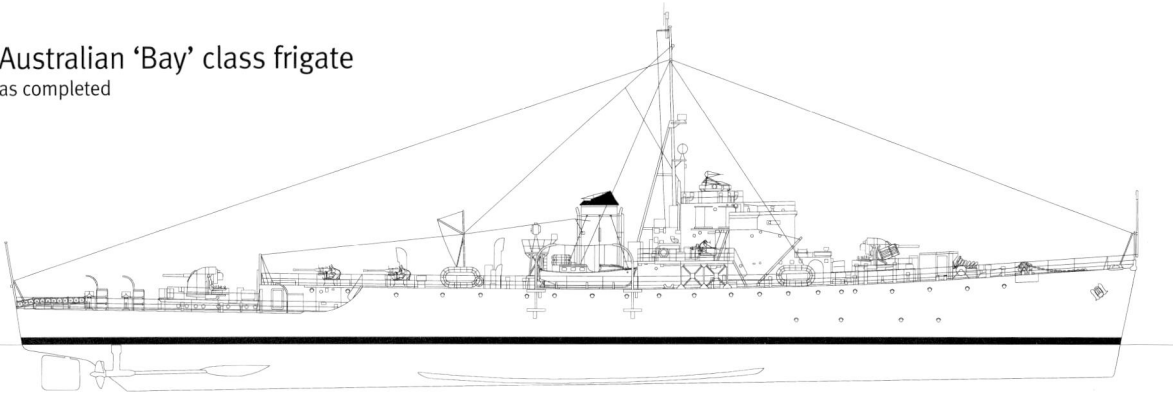

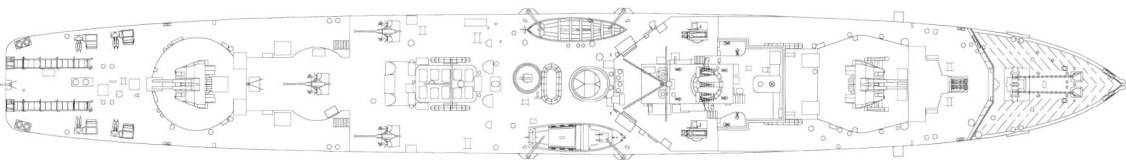

Ex-US *Evarts* type
as taken over as RN 'Captain' class

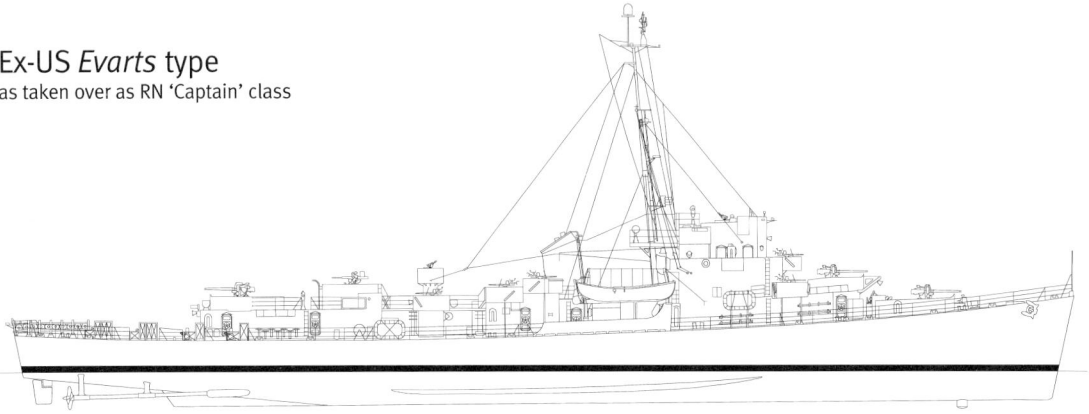

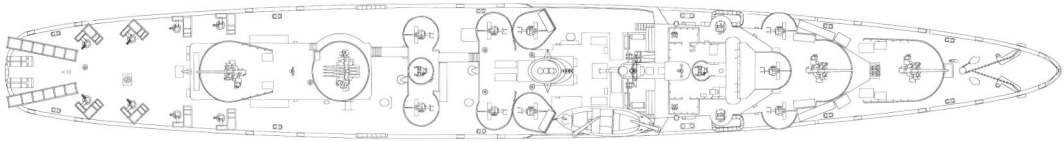

HMS *Goodall*
ex-US *Evarts* type, as taken over as RN 'Captain' class

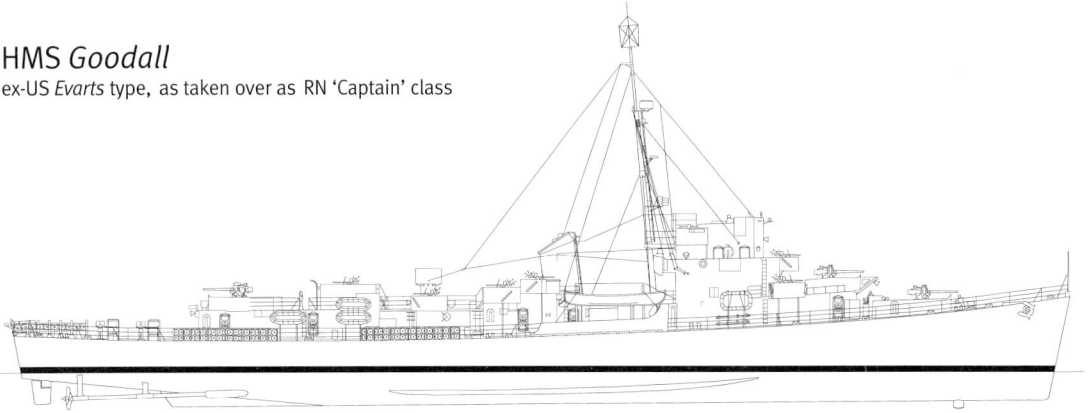

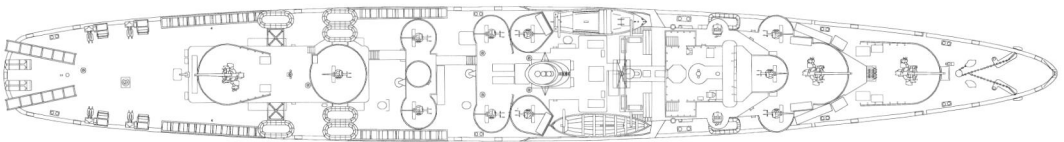

US *Buckley* class
as in USN service

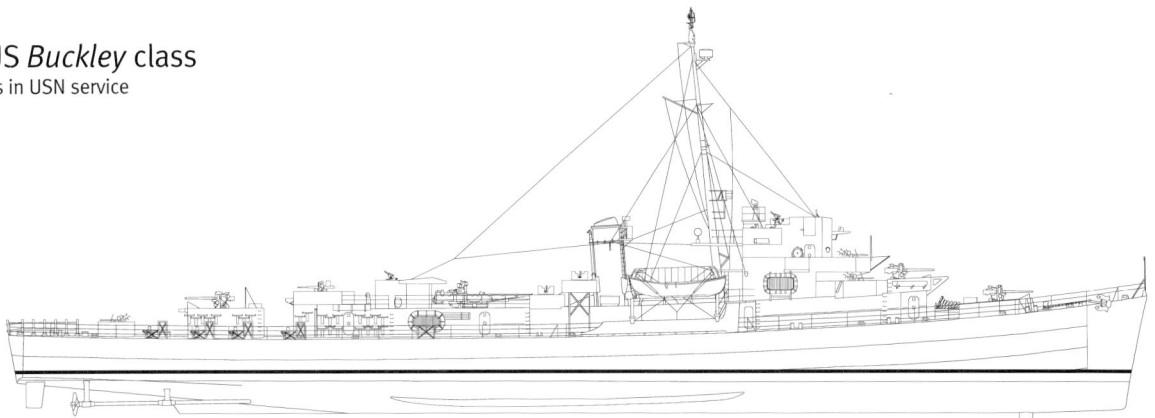

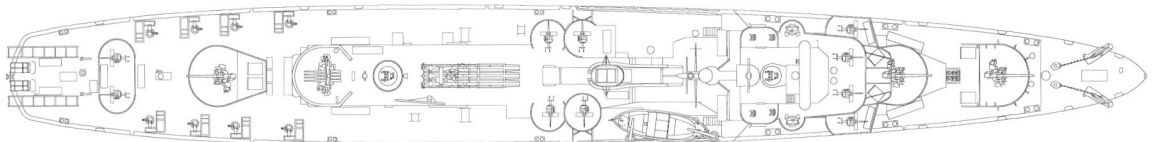

Ex-US *Buckley* type
as taken over as RN 'Captain' class

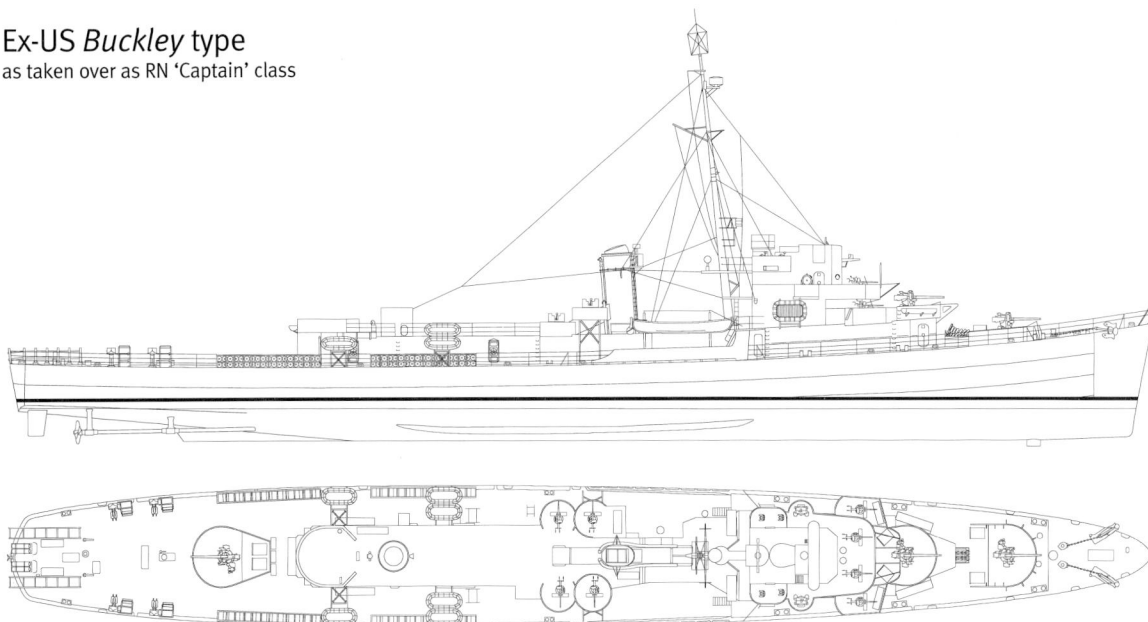

USCG 'Lake' class
1929

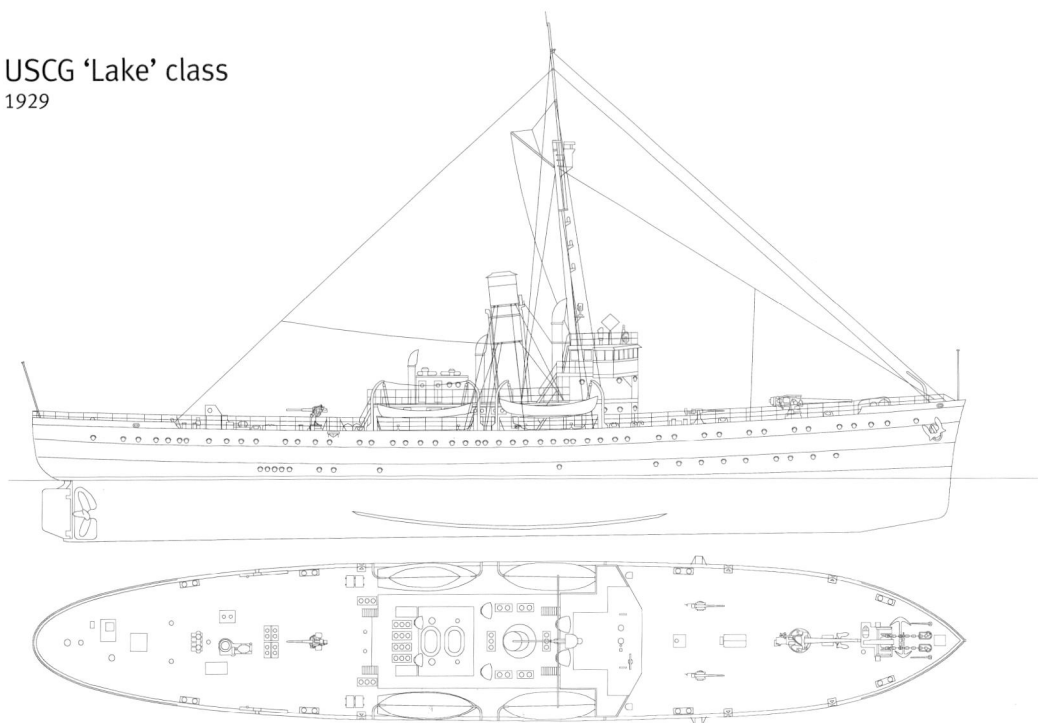

HMS *Totland*
ex-USCG 'Lake' class,
RN *Banff* class, 1943

*(All drawings by
George Richardson)*

Selected References

BIBLIOGRAPHY

Allied Escort Ships of World War II, by Peter Elliott (Macdonald and Jane's Publishers, 1977)

Anatomy of the Ship: The Destroyer Escort England, by Al Ross (Conway Maritime Press, 1985)

Anti-Submarine Warfare, by David Owen (Seaforth Publishing, 2007)

Atlantic Escorts, by David K Brown (Seaforth Publishing, 2007)

Black Swan Class Sloops, by Les Brown (Seaforth Publishing, 2020)

British and Commonwealth Warship Camouflage of WWII, (Destroyers, Frigates, Escorts), by Malcolm Wright (Seaforth Publishing, 2014)

British and Empire Warships of the Second World War, by H T Lenton (Greenhill Books, 1998)

British Destroyers & Frigates, by Norman Friedman (Seaforth Publishing, 2006)

Conway's All the World's Fighting Ships 1906–1921, edited by Robert Gardiner (Conway Maritime Press, 1985)

Conway's All The World's Fighting Ships 1922–1946, edited by Robert Gardiner (Conway Maritime Press, 1980)

Destroyer Escorts in Action, by Al Adcock (Squadron/Signal Publications, 1997)

Frigates of the Royal Canadian Navy 1943–1974, by Ken Macpherson (Distributed by Tri-Service Press, 1989)

Frigates, Sloops, & Patrol Vessels of the Royal Navy 1900 to date, by M P Coker (Westmorland Gazette, 1985)

River Class Frigates and the Battle of the Atlantic, by Brian Lavery (National Maritime Museum, 2006)

Royal Navy Handbook 1939–1945, by David Wragg (Sutton Publishing, 2005)

Sloops 1926–1946, by Arnold Hague (World Ship Society, 1993)

The Buckley-Class Destroyer Escorts, by Bruce Hampton Franklin (Naval Institute Press, 1999)

The Captain Class Frigates in the Second World War, by Donald Collingwood (Leo Cooper, 1998)

The Patrol Frigate Story, by David Hendrickson (Fortis Publishing, 2011)

US Destroyers, by Norman Friedman (Naval Institute Press, 2004)

Warship Perspectives – Camouflage Volume Two, Royal Navy 1942, by Alan Raven (WR Press, 2001)

Warship Perspectives – Camouflage Volume Three, Royal Navy 1943–1944, by Alan Raven (WR Press, 2001)

Warship Perspectives – Camouflage Volume Four, Royal Navy Supplemental, by Alan Raven (WR Press, 2003)

WW2 Fact Files: British Escort Ships, by H T Lenton (Macdonald and Jane's Publishers, 1974)

MODELLING WEBSITES

www.ajmmodels.pl – Polish manufacturer of resin kits and accessories

https://www.atlanticmodels.net – UK manufacturer of resin kits and etched brass detail sets, including many kits previously produced by White Ensign Models (UK).

https://blackcatmodels.eu – French manufacturer of resin kits and 3D printed accessories

www.deansmarine.co.uk – UK manufacturer of radio control kits and accessories

www.ironshipwrights.com – US manufacturer of resin kits

www.neptunia-hobbies.com – UK manufacturer of card models

www.starling-models.co.uk – UK manufacturer of resin kits and etched brass detail sets, and supplier of a wide range of plastic and resin kits and accessories from international manufacturers.

www.tomsmodelworks.com – US manufacturer of etched brass accessories

www.whiteensignmodels.com – US manufacturer of etched brass accessories

Right: *Opossum* on 14 July 1945, a late-war example of the Modified *Black Swan* class with a lattice mast and enhanced AA outfit including two twin 40mm Bofors on Hazemeyer mountings on a platform aft of the funnel and two twin power-operated 20mm mountings on the quarterdeck.